Time [illegible] Me a [illegible] Someday

Best Wishes

Mike Philpott

Mike Philpott

Trailing The Vapors

Cover Design by Suzanne Krasnowska

ISBN 978-1-9162159-0-0

Acknowledgements

With thanks to Dave, Steve, Michael, Dan, Ed, Branka, Shaun, Evan and Bobby for their valuable contributions. Also to Jeanette, Anna, Tim, Suzanne, Elaine, Sally and Owen for all of the help. And of course to Beccy, Joe and Robin.

And to the extended Vapors Family, so numerous and widespread, and so many unknown by name, but especially of course to Jacquie and Jacqui, Kev, Colin, Pete, Jane, Mandy, Rich, Rob, Matt, Graham, Karen and Jen.

For Sarah Kent

Introduction

"Does Mike want anything to eat before we set off?" A crisp, chirpy voice yells from somewhere upstairs, shrill but distinctively cheerful, unmistakably Yorkshire and unmistakably commanding her addressee into action rather than actually asking him a direct question.

I'm relaxing, reclining on a smart dark leather sofa, one of two arranged at right angles in a clean, spacious, lightly coloured lounge overlooking the back garden of a detached house on the better side of Worthing. The welcoming, tidy room is brought to life spectacularly by large panoramic French windows that invite the winter sun to flood through, igniting reflections that sparkle from the recently decorated Christmas tree. Three of us chat idly, two of our number stretched out on one of the sofas, the owner of the house laying back diagonally across, and dwarfed by, the other. Various faceless contributors interrupt us occasionally from the rolling TV news show flickering away in the corner, earnestly trying to explain the complexities and calculations of that week's forthcoming parliamentary Brexit vote.

Her husband responds from his prone position on the opposite sofa, repeating her question directly to me, word-for-word, politely but with a wry grin cracking his lips and an amused sparkle in his eyes, acknowledgement of a resigned but contented acceptance of his status in the domestic hierarchy. I smile a grateful nod, and he springs up and walks to the kitchen, his short, slight stature, topped with slightly thinned greying hair, still grown to regulation early 80s pop star length, returning with a steaming bowl of cold-weather-warming chilli. "Would you like a cracker with that?" he asks in a faintly croaky, softly spoken clipped suburban South-East accent whilst placing a box on the table next to me, deliberately and carefully removing the lid without waiting for a response.

The well-groomed, shaven-headed man on the sofa next to me, casually dressed in a smart designer top and perfectly creased big brand trousers, chuckles. "Did you ever imagine," he laughs out loud in that most stereotypical of Birmingham accents, all nose and vowels but seemingly deliberately pronounced in near slow-motion "that when you were leaping like a lunatic around the Marquee club as a teenager whilst Dave played onstage, 40 years later he'd be feeding you Sunday lunch in his front room?"

I grin, and he continues "Or that you would have flown to New York City with him and his band to see them play some gigs either?!"

The three of us laugh, engaging in a quick-fire round of "things we never expected to happen 40 years ago", whilst I scoff my surprise but hugely welcome lunch and the further drudgeries of the late 2018 political impasse drone away in the background.

A few minutes subsequent to her over-the-bannister distant instruction dressed up as a question, Branka Fenton arrives downstairs. Her long dark hair is tied back purposefully, shades balanced on her forehead poised and ready to deflect the low in the sky December sunshine we will be chasing west on our forthcoming drive. All bustle and big personality, she casts a busy eye around the room, sweeps up her bag and a couple of CDs, and declares that it's time to leave. We move slowly outside and get into two cars ready for the relatively short trip to Southampton. I clamber into the passenger seat of the family car that Branka will drive, whilst Dave eases himself into the gleaming sports car belonging to my erstwhile sofa-companion, modern-day band manager, Shaun Modern. Whilst Dave's wife had very obviously been in charge inside the house, Shaun quickly takes over operations once we hit the road and the day's focus turns from relaxation to business, and to bringing the myriad constituent parts of that evening's gig featuring Dave's reformed band, The Vapors, together in the right place at the right time.

******

Numerous Internet articles, and a substantial amount of printed and recorded pieces, will variously describe The Vapors as a late 1970s/early 1980s Post-Punk, Power Pop or New Wave band. The reader or listener will then be told that the band are best known for their worldwide hit "Turning Japanese" and almost certainly be informed that they were discovered by The Jam's Bruce Foxton who subsequently became their manager in partnership with Paul Weller's father John. Their split, in 1981, after the recording of two studio albums and the release of six singles, will also inevitably be mentioned, and if the article in question has either been written or updated in recent years, it will state that the band reformed to play a series of gigs in 2016 and remain together as an active, professional, working unit today.

Whilst some other slightly more in-depth interviews and blog articles exist, the impression gleaned by the casual reader will most likely be that The Vapors are a small footnote in rock and roll history. This may or may not be a reasonable conclusion to draw, but for myself and a significant number of others, both in the United Kingdom and across the world, they represent more than just another band. They may only have produced two albums (at the time of writing), they may only have existed as a going concern for six of the fifty-five years that I have been around, and for the majority of people who are actually aware of their work they may well represent no more than a classic case of the one-hit-wonder.

However, their music, and the culture that existed around them first time round, and which has been revitalised and expanded upon since they reformed in 2016, transcends music and forms a hugely important part of the lives of some of us in our own little corners of the world. There are a million reasons to be despondent about the current state of humanity, and one guitar-based pop band won't change that. But the existence of a tiny subset of Planet Earth's population, fondly branded "The Vapors Family" by those of us who make a point of travelling the length and breadth of the UK (and more recently further afield) to support the band and their music, and the friendships and bonds we have formed is, in some small way, truly life-affirming.

This book is neither an end-to-end detailed history of The Vapors, nor a detailed memoir of the many areas of my own life, but it does tell the story of how and why one band became, and remain, such an important part not just of my world, but of many others' like mine. It tells the story of how this group of musicians and their family, friends and fans, all represent a constituent part in the make-up of a suburban boy who grew up in the 1970s, and why they impact, and are entwined with, his life to this day.

I was raised in the relatively safe, but eternally dull, satellite town comfort offered by the commuter belt of South-East England. I happened to live in Haywards Heath, in Sussex, sandwiched between the never quite reachable international end-point promise and glamour offered by Gatwick Airport to the north and the perpetually seedy but equally exciting vibrance of Brighton to the south. But I could have been in Farnborough, or Slough, or Hemel Hempstead, or Harlow, or Chelmsford, or Maidstone, or any other number of similar places, and I doubt it would have felt much different. There will be many who identify with the life passage I describe in this book, and I am sure will recognise similarities in their own trips. Music may or may not have been the vehicle for their own journeys, and even if it was, they will probably not have the same affinity for the music of The Vapors. But they will all have their equivalent.

******

Technology assists and intervenes with equal measures of helpfulness and irritation as we head west along the South Coast on the A27.

Dave rings from his mobile to remind Branka to make a note of the mileage before setting out, but she misses the call and receives it on voicemail several miles too late.

"At the roundabout, take the second exit towards Portsmouth and Southampton" barks the Satnav for the fifteenth time.

Shaun calls to check our ETA as we get close to the venue, switch off the Satnav and immediately skirt the turning that should have taken us over the huge, unmissable structure of the bridge that spans the wide expanse of the River Itchen.

Technology dismissed, we correct our mistake and arrive at The 1865, a medium-sized rock club in Southampton city centre where Shaun and Dave have already arrived. The December sun has given way to late, lazy Sunday winter afternoon empty city stark concrete bleakness and crisp twilight chill, but the cheerful atmosphere remains unchecked as we step out of our cars and stroll into the venue. We are joined by another Vapors stalwart, technical master and roadie-in-chief Tim Cox, whose ever-present shorts and distinctive baseball-capped bald head are as recognisable to fans now as his ever-present shorts and distinctive flowing long curly hair had been the first-time round.

Drummer Michael Bowes arrives, a dreadlocked gentle giant of a man whose relaxed demeanour and permanent smile is only broken when the band is on stage, at which point he turns into a sweaty whirlwind of physicality and the smile becomes even wider and even more permanent.

Bassist Steve Smith walks into the empty auditorium, along with lead guitarist Ed Bazalgette, two old bandmates who have remained lifetime friends and become two reunited bandmates. The youngest of the band's original line-up, Ed's still youthful grin belies a confidence borne of a successful career as a TV director, his first Vapors incarnation prototype 80s big hair also having given way to his modern-day bald head. Steve's uncut long curls provide enough hair for both of them, his less youthful but equally as confident and friendly grin shining through a slowly-receding hangover, one of many that have undoubtedly contributed to his life-well-lived appearance that stems from a career clearly enjoyed to its full potential as a professional musician and sound engineer.

Instruments, amps, and merchandise are unloaded. The stage is built, the soundchecks completed and the t-shirts laid out on the night's makeshift merchandise stall. Setlists are produced and taped down, and the mood continues its shift from relaxed preparation to focussed professionalism. The band, now in fully-fledged performance mode, retreat to the sanctity of their dressing room, and the rest of us retire to the nearest decent-looking pub for the by now traditional pre-gig Vapors Family meet-up.

I spent 18 months of my teenage life attending Vapors gigs, and 35 years of my adult life reminiscing fondly about them. The familiarity and regularity of modern-day Vapors concerts since the band's rebirth in 2016 is nostalgic, current, optimistic, comforting and exciting in equal measures, and this one, in late 2018, is no different.

This Is It; This Is All I Need

I am a music fan. I've always been a music fan. At some points in the last fifty-five years music has been a massively important part of my life, at other points it's been little more than a peripheral interest. But it's always been there, and I've always been a music fan.

My parents were both musicians. I grew up accustomed to the seemingly endless background noise of middle-class kids displaying an extraordinarily staggering range of skill levels as they battled their way up and down the keyboard under my mother's piano-teaching tuition. My father produced concerts and other live musical performances of some distinction for BBC Radios 2 and 3.

Outside of their professional and work environments, my parents both had a deep and passionate love for music that governed their lives and shaped the early development of my two sisters, Suzi and Jeanette, 2 and 5 years younger than me respectively, and myself. They would sing in choirs, my mother would provide piano accompaniment, my father would fill up a succession of flimsily built English 70s family estate cars with his double bass and scoot off to who knows where for appearances with string quartets, orchestras and a multitude of other assorted-sized and styled ensembles. When he wasn't playing, he would twirl a stick around mysteriously with a fixed, encouraging smile on his face and conduct choirs within which my mother would either be singing with an equally bizarre set smile, or for whom she would be carrying out the aforementioned piano duties. And most spectacularly of all, from a very early age my sisters and I would regularly be wheeled off to church halls in unpronounceable villages across Sussex to savour concerts performed by the Martlet Singers, an eight-piece vocal group to which both of my parents belonged. The group would perform acapella Elizabethan madrigals and other long-lost delights from yesteryear, interspersed with poetry readings, and recorder recitals performed by a handful of their delightful children, yours truly included.

So music was the norm for us as children. Whether it be emanating from the radio, the monolithic "gramophone unit" that seemed to occupy half of the living room of our suburban family home, or whether it was as part of an audience at any number of rehearsals or concerts that my parents were engaged with, it was always there.

And it was OK. I certainly didn't share my parents' deep love of classical music, and although it consumed an enormous amount of childhood time that could otherwise have been spent playing football like all the normal kids seemed to be able to do, it never seemed like too much of a problem. It was a big part of my experience of growing up, and it was OK.

But it didn't excite, or even enthuse. Nonetheless, I guess it helped spawn the appreciation and respect that I retain for musicians to this day and helped engender the love of music which was later to burn so strongly within me.

And at the age of eight I discovered Pop Music.

My first musical awakening came in the unlikely form of Chuck Berry performing his novelty hit "My Ding-a-Ling". As an eight-year-old I was vaguely aware of the existence of this thing called Pop Music, kids would occasionally talk about it at school or sing lines from the hits of the day in the playground ("Chirpy Chirpy Cheep Cheep" springs eerily to mind) but it all seemed faintly ridiculous to me. My parents were hardly puritanical bible-belt style conservatives (of the sort I do recall quite clearly as being prevalent in the Mid-Sussex hinterlands during my formative years) who believed that rock and roll and the devil were inextricably connected, but I was left in no doubt that Pop Music was trivial nonsense, and not really worth bothering with. (Even though, later in life, I learnt that my father had witnessed a very early Beatles session recording at the BBC and felt at the time that they "could go on to be quite successful").

At that point in my development I had yet to discover all that rock and roll had to offer, however I did consider myself very grown up and cultured in some ways, and this had led to an early love for the undoubted comedy genius that was Eric Sykes. The "Sykes" TV show of the time aired at 8.00pm on Thursday evenings, and I had somehow managed to negotiate staying up late to watch it one week. This was probably in part due to my mother's sympathy with my inability to watch normal kids' TV in those days because of the never-ending stream of pupils receiving tuition with their scales and arpeggios on the piano, which just happened to be in the same room as the television.

Settling down in front of the TV to watch my new favourite sitcom one November evening in 1972, I happened to catch the last few minutes of "Top of the Pops". Chuck

Berry was at number one with the song, and I found it amusing. Not in the same way that I later learnt that adults found it amusing, but nonetheless, it was my eye-opener to the fact that maybe this Pop Music thing wasn't so bad after all.

I didn't really know at that stage how the chart structure worked, so the following week I tuned in to "Top of the Pops" right from the beginning, hoping I might catch that amusing song one more time. I guess it had slipped down the chart, because I was to be disappointed, but what I did see was a swirling mass of colour, larger than life characters, tunes that were instantly catchy in a way that the Martlet Singers' renditions never had been, and a bunch of people who seemed to be having an enormous amount of fun.

I was hooked.

The next few years would be spent religiously watching "Top of the Pops" and whatever other (very limited in those days) TV programmes broadcasting the popular tunes and acts of the day I could find. I took the tiny family transistor radio from the kitchen on permanent loan, tuning in to Radio 1 at every available opportunity, and inventing my very own prototype Walkman for car journeys. This involved sitting on the back seat leaning against the window with the radio wedged between my ear and the glass, playing at a low enough volume so as to be audible only to myself. (I was later to adapt this model when I became the proud owner of my first cassette machine, but in reality, the subsequent invention of the actual Walkman was probably a good thing in terms of preventing the need for some form of corrective neck therapy).

I watched and listened in wonder to the likes of The Sweet, T-Rex, David Bowie, Slade and the now airbrushed-from-history Gary Glitter. Without realising it at the time, I had become a glam-rock fan, but I was fascinated too by other, diverse sounds I heard without knowing necessarily what I was listening to. Country rock hits, novelty records, early heavy metal acts, classic pop hits like "Seasons in the Sun" by Terry Jacks all became part of the whirl of excitement that I was experiencing. Bands like Sparks and Queen came along and just added to the visual and aural wonder of it all and I began to actively seek out musicians and artists rather than just letting them fall out of the television at me.

Radio 1 provided a perfect audio supplement to the colour and visual wonder that was on display at 7.30 on BBC1 every Thursday night, and became my single biggest influence in terms of musical education throughout the early 1970s. I learnt how the chart worked, and tuned in with excitement to the Top 30 (as it was then) update shows every week, with an anticipation level that very little in later life has even come close to matching. Knowing who had won the latest Slade vs. Gary Glitter race to number one seemed to be just about the most important thing that life had to offer.

The more I listened to the radio, the more I began to realise that contemporary music had even more to offer than what I saw on the television once a week. And more importantly, that Pop Music hadn't actually begun with Chuck Berry releasing a throwaway live recording in November 1972.

Through radio programmes with such gravitas and authority as "Tony Blackburn's Golden Hour" I learnt about something called "The Fifties". And even better, "The Sixties". The first Beatles song I remember consciously hearing was "She Loves You" and here was yet another facet of this wonderful thing called Pop Music for me to fall in love with. When the girl from over the road popped round one day with copies of the Red and Blue Beatles compilations that were actually capable of being played on that gramophone, through actual speakers, at high volume, I genuinely believed that I would never need to listen to anything else ever again. These four treasures of vinyl that lasted for HOURS that she had been given for her birthday (she was a year older than me, and consequently highly cultured) would probably keep me going for ever.

But of course, my thirst was unquenched, and through other radio programmes, other kids at school (or more likely other kids' parents, but via those kids) I began to discover more wonders from the depths of history such as The Who, The Rolling Stones, The Kinks and many other bands whose music I retain a deep love for to this day.

In my last year at Harlands, then as now a respected and successful primary school, one of the cooler teachers ran a music club at lunchtimes. I wasn't lucky enough to have been placed in Mr Turner's class, but those who had been spoke with nothing other than wide-eyed 10-year-old wonder and amazement at this slightly balding, cheeky-grinned, larger than life Scouser. He was full of footballing tales about his beloved reds, a team that those of us who had also become football fanatics in our lesser years were only too aware of, despite the fact that Liverpool may have been on the other side of the world from Haywards Heath back then, in so many ways.

Our paths criss-crossed continually during those last few months of junior school, however. Mr Turner was also the games teacher and ran football and cricket teams within which I was an enthusiastic participant. He also afforded me the highest honour I could imagine just after my eleventh birthday when I was made one of four team captains for the end of year sports day, an athletic pinnacle that was only challenged briefly in my late teens with some moderate cricketing success. His unwavering care, humour and total attention to his charges were universally loved by the kids at school, and to this day I am still in regular contact with two who were lucky enough to have had him as their full time teacher and speak with nothing but praise of their time under his tutelage: one of these being my sister Suzi who was in his class two years after I had moved on to secondary school, and the other being a girl called Sally. Sally had moved to the area that year, and she and I progressed through both secondary school and sixth form in parallel, although we were never friends or really members of the same peer groups. We had very different paths through our adolescences, and aged 18 set off on our tangentially diverse life trips as did hundreds of other vague acquaintances who I'd never got to know and would never see again. Sally, however, was to return into my life many, many years later in the most unexpected of fashions.

So Mr Turner's announcement that he would bring in some of his records and play them at lunchtimes to anyone who fancied turning up was as large a magnet as any offer anyone had ever made. I remember countless contemporaries cramming into his classroom on many such occasions, where he'd play us Eric Clapton, Free, early Led

Zeppelin and many others who weren't appearing regularly on "Top of the Pops" or daytime Radio 1 at the time, as well as tunes from what would have been his own formative years. The highlights, of course, were the bands from his distant but wondrous hometown, which were always introduced to us with a tale or two, and it seemed entirely plausible to us for a while that Mr Turner himself may have been the fifth Beatle.

The musical pit was bottomless, and it just seemed to get more and more exciting as every week passed, and although moving up to secondary school was a daunting prospect after the near-universal happiness of Harlands, it was a step that I was ready for, and needed to take because as much as any other factor, it could only serve to broaden my ever-expanding horizons of popular culture.

In September 1975 I started at Haywards Heath School. The stark, fifties-built patchwork of glass and brick blocks, hastily sticky-plastered prefabricated population boom huts and not so temporary buildings stood out on the side of a hill in the middle of an aspirational post-war housing estate that had been cemented onto the town on its western side. The establishment has had a chameleon-like existence, initially being opened in the late 1950s as a Grammar School, before converting to Comprehensive status before I arrived. Immediately upon my arrival, a decision was made to create a Sixth-Form college on the site, and my year group was therefore the final intake for the school. I have no idea of the psychological effect that only ever having older kids surrounding us had on myself or my peers, however we had to negotiate the entirety of the years between eleven and seventeen being the youngest kids in the school. After my departure the place thrived as a college before merging with institutions in Crawley to become Central Sussex College. Recently, however, it has been closed and is currently just another ugly, security-gated, weed surrounded sign of the times eyesore, having fallen victim to its parent company's financial mismanagement. It is still prominent on its hill, and still as familiar a journey-progression landmark to commuters on the London to Brighton line as Croydon's concrete sprawl and Gatwick Airport's bustle, and thankfully for the teenagers of Mid-Sussex is due to reopen in 2020 after Chichester College Group's rescue merger with Central Sussex College.

Suddenly I was surrounded by an enormous number of new and interesting classmates, some of whom came from as far away as the other end of town. The time-honoured icebreaker "So what sort of music are you into?", which has served me so well throughout life, became a regular conversation opener in those first few weeks.

And the floodgates of pop were thrown even more widely open. I struck a deal with a new friend (who I knew was cool because he was a goalkeeper) to pay 5p a week for 10 weeks for a copy of something called "Tubular Bells" which he assured me was a classic album that I would love. (This didn't quite explain why he was so happy to part with it, but that didn't seem too important at the time). And better still he was happy to hand it over to me after only the first payment. I can't remember the exact date, but at some point in September or October of 1975 I became the proud owner of my first ever record. It might have been second-hand, but it was mine. All mine.

I had other records in my fledgling collection. My father would occasionally arrive home with a random assortment of vinyl that I assume had landed on his desk at work (or that of one of his colleagues) as promotional material. (I realised later that they were all on one of two record labels). He'd walk in through the kitchen door at 7.20pm every night (the trains always ran on time back then of course) where I may or may not have been sat at the family's red Formica table doing my homework. He'd get them out of his briefcase, slap them down on the table and state with a grin that he "thought you might like these." I never did of course, although I do remember one of them being a Santana single that I thought was probably quite cool as I had at least heard of them. But mostly they comprised of such long-lost classics as the debut album by "Kojak" star Telly Savalas and were treated with the scorn that they probably deserved.

My parents, with hindsight, had succumbed to the reality quite early on that my musical tastes were not quite the same as theirs, and they had obviously made a conscious decision to embrace and support my journey into pop. My mother would make a weekly pilgrimage into the living room once (and only once) during every edition of "Top of the Pops", perform a strange little wiggle of a dance that involved sticking her arms down straight with her hands outstretched at right angles, move her neck about a little and utter that immortal, timeless participatory parental phrase "Hey, this one's got a good beat." Whereupon she would leave the room again as quickly as she could. My father studied for, and successfully obtained, an Open University degree in I'm not quite sure what, which involved, amongst other things, him having to listen to music with a social narrative. I remember him deliberately inviting me into the sanctity of the living room (which was otherwise off-limits when he was studying) one evening to listen to Bob Marley with him, presumably because it fitted the bill of sharing something with his son that I would appreciate. In fact, as a twelve-year-old I probably wasn't quite ready for Bob Marley, but I certainly grew to love his music when I was older, once my tastes had refined and expanded.

So although the vinyl treasures that my father brought home once in a while would be placed in neat vertical storage compartments deep in the bosom of the gramophone unit's wooden infrastructure, they didn't feel like MY records. Mike Oldfield's multi-tracked, multi-instrumental masterpiece, on the other hand, did. I'd paid for this out of my hard-earned pocket money, and I had a beautiful piece of circular 12-inch plastic to call my own. My family must have been driven mad by the ghostly sounds of the first side of that album, which was probably played three or four times a day at weekends for the next few months, but I didn't care, I owned a record.

Gradually my continual awakening to the wider wonders of Pop Music, which I was now beginning to understand was comprised of so many different styles and genres, continued and evolved. Many of my new schoolmates had incredibly cool big brothers and sisters, and I was introduced to epoch defining marvels such as Barclay James Harvest and Emerson, Lake and Palmer. I don't think I ever heard an ELP track until much later in life, but I knew they were cool because someone's 14-year-old brother was into them, and that was good enough for me. Their name got scrawled on to my pencil case along with whatever other artists of the day I was into for the lifespan of each particular pencil case.

And so it grew and grew.

But then, one day, my world came crashing down.

Don't Like Your Damned New Rose

My parents weren't Daily Mail readers. This book isn't about politics, and in fact over the years I know for sure that the views of both of my parents liberalised to quite some extent. Nevertheless, it is accurate to state that in the early 1970s they represented the fairly typical Conservative electorate (with a relatively large "C") of the sort stereotypically associated with South East towns to this day.

And although they weren't Daily Mail readers (in fact the only newspapers we'd ever see in our house were editions of the Sunday Observer), I am sure a number of their peer group and friends in Mid-Sussex were. So it is probably fair to say that a sizeable amount of the information I received concerning popular culture, and society in general, came from that unique end of the journalistic spectrum.

I recall quite clearly the day my mother asked me if I had heard of something called Punk Pop (her words). When I told her that I hadn't, she began to tell me, with what I genuinely remember as a very worried look upon her face, that there was a group of people "out there" (mainly she thought in London but she wasn't sure), who had decided that they didn't like Pop Music and they were going to destroy it.

I was terrified! What the hell did this mean? Who the hell were these people and what right could they possibly have to want to try and destroy this thing that I had invested so much of my time and effort into, and of which I had become such an aficionado?

And it got worse. I went in to school the next day and confided in some of my friends exactly what I had been told, desperate for them to reassure me that no, she must have got that wrong, it was probably nothing, and that even if this thing was real it wouldn't work. Any crumb of comfort would have helped, but no such crumb was offered. My friends too, it seemed, had heard about this phenomenon, and it was even worse than I thought! These Punk Rockers (my friends were at least quickly able to correct the terminology) apparently dressed a bit funny and were going to force everyone else to do so as well! They were going to smash society from the top to the bottom, and everything that we had grown to love and hold so dear as well off 12-year-old suburban kids was going to be wrested away from us.

I couldn't sleep for days. I was less worried about the imminent breakdown of society than the impending loss of my beloved Pop Music, but it was a stressful time of uncertainty for me, and every day I would nervously tune in to Radio 1, or even the BBC News, to see if the destruction of my seemingly perfect little world had yet begun.

And then, in June 1977, the BBC were responsible for a musical awakening that was to be a thousand times more thunderous than Chuck Berry had managed with his ding-a-ling five years previously. Despite the ongoing non-obliteration of my world I would still tune in with slight trepidation every week to "Top of the Pops" just to reassure myself that the very fabric of civilisation as I knew it was still intact.

And one week, the also airbrushed-from-history Jimmy Savile was presenting the show, and in his unmistakable, even back then tiresome style, casually informed viewers that we were about to witness "Something you've never seen before...this...here...is The Stranglers..."

"BOOOGGGIIIEEEEE!" yelled a menacing but incredibly cool looking dude in a black jacket, followed by a cursory and dismissive "woogie".

The next two minutes and fifty seconds did more than change my life. They defined what a big part of the next 42 years (and counting, I hope) would be framed by.

I was transfixed. A bunch of surly looking young(ish) men came kicking and screaming out of the television at me.

Whoever these guys were launched into a raucous up-beat rock and roll song that seemed somehow different to anything that had ever gone before from the very first chord.

Jean-Jacques Burnel snarled into the microphone packing more attitude than most men will muster during a whole lifetime. Hugh Cornwell scowled at the camera whilst treating his bass guitar simultaneously as a weapon and a punchbag (it was only recently, after looking up this recording on YouTube, that I realised the pair had swapped instruments for this pre-recorded and mimed performance). Dave Greenfield was sat at the side of the stage bullying his keyboards in a way that I never imagined possible from all that I had learned growing up with the constant backdrop of Grade 1 piano pupils learning their scales. Jet Black banged the drums and stared into the distance with a "Don't come near me" face that looked like he meant it, and which didn't budge for the whole performance, or probably ever for that matter.

And the colossal, immense, sum of the parts thumped out of the 70s television perched on its spindly legs in the corner. A monstrous rock song ensued that within 10 seconds of starting was begging for the volume to be turned up to full (it would have been if such luxuries as remote control had existed back then).

I had never seen, or heard, anything like it. There was no such thing as video or any other form of playback device available to me in those days, but if there had been, I'd have stopped everything right there and spent the night re-running what I had just witnessed. Once again, I couldn't sleep, but this time it was out of sheer excitement. It had started as just another Thursday, just another "Top of the Pops", and ended in a haze of wonder. Who the hell were those guys? What the hell was that song? Above all, what the hell was that all about?

The weekly Friday morning discussion at school was different that week.

"Did you see 'Top of the Pops' last night?"

"Yeah, it was alright wasn't it!"

"Who were that band that were on, all dressed in black, you know, The Stranglers or something I think they were called?"

"Oh yeah, they were quite good weren't they, they're a Punk Rock band."

My head whirled. "Hold it!" I thought, "Stop right there, say that again?"

That was Punk Rock? That was what I've been living in fear of all these months? That is what I needed to be so careful to avoid?

Bring it on!

Things gathered pace. Unbeknown to me up until that point The Sex Pistols had stormed up the charts with "God Save The Queen". Unbeknown of course because the BBC had decided to ban the record. The concealing of this song from the masses at the time seems so trivial now, and certainly when set alongside the subsequent airbrushing of previously referenced contemporaries such as Gary Glitter and Jimmy Savile also seems unpalatable and ludicrous. But such was the mood of the middle classes back then that the attitude of the authorities would probably sadly have treated the severity of those characters' misdemeanours, had they been publicly known, as no more than the equal of the unacceptability of the Pistols' vitriol.

No matter. "Pretty Vacant" quickly followed and The Sex Pistols were quickly made accessible on mainstream radio. The Stranglers had taught me within the space of three minutes that my long, unfounded fear of Punk Rock had been misplaced, but quickly the sheer depth and quantity of what was out there was becoming clear, and it became hugely exciting.

The next six months brought a range and variety of sounds all broadly described by music historians as fitting the punk label, but that with hindsight spanned all sorts of musical styles. It is interesting to look back at the big hits of the second half of 1977. A perfunctory glance at Wikipedia's listing of top ten singles from that period only begins to tell the story. The few entries up until the end of that year that would seemingly fit the bill are The Pistols and The Stranglers (3 singles each), Eddie and the Hot Rods (billed as "The Rods" on the credits for "Do Anything You Wanna Do" in its top ten incarnation), the Tom Robinson Band and, further leftfield, Jonathan Richman and the Modern Lovers.

Outside the top ten was a different story, and during that period countless other contemporary marvels were materialising. The Damned, Buzzcocks, Elvis Costello, The Ramones, Talking Heads, XTC, The Boomtown Rats, Nick Lowe, Ian Dury; the roll call of acts breaking into the mainstream and into my world extended and grew, and the list of musicians creating music that thrilled felt like it was infinite. The Jam appeared on my radar, closely followed by The Clash, and after six short months the landscape was permanently reformatted. I was able to define my exact musical tastes and loves very precisely for the first time to anyone who cared to listen and also made a point of doing so to many who didn't.

I was a punk. Albeit one kitted out by my parents in school uniform during the week and Marks and Spencer casual wear at weekends, with a sensible haircut, a bedroom of my own in a warm, comfortable house and one showing early academic promise and studying diligently. But I was a punk nonetheless, because I KNEW I was.

As was my latest friend, a new kid at school who had moved down from actual London, a place where I assumed by that point that everyone was now a punk, revelling in their squalor and living their free, anarchic lives. No matter that he actually came from a part of Dulwich that probably made Haywards Heath look like a rundown inner-city slum riddled with deprivation by comparison, he was from

London and he was a punk, because he told me that he was, and that was good enough for me.

One Friday he mentioned that his mum was going to buy him a black T-shirt, and how she had asked if she should get me one too. They were available at the local market for 99p each, so it seemed to be too good an opportunity to miss. She duly delivered, and on the following Monday I rushed home from school to put on my new cool accessory, and there I was in the mirror, not only being a punk, but actually dressing like one too. I never quite progressed through to the safety pins or bondage trousers (it would be 1980 before I was brave enough to get my hair shaved off, and 1982 before I plucked up the courage to get my ear pierced), but at least I could now look the part when playing air guitar along to the still ever-present transistor radio.

The snowballing of my musical surface area continued unabated. The trusty transistor was now smuggled down the side of my bed every weekday night in preparation for secretly listening to John Peel. I doubt I ever managed to stay awake long enough to hear the end of any of his broadcasts, but the sheer number of bands and tunes from those days that I remember, or that I have since rediscovered, is staggering.

And then there were record shops.

My eldest sister and I would often amuse ourselves whilst visiting the sweet shop with our pocket money by setting ourselves the task of walking into, and speaking to somebody within, every shop in South Road, the Fifth Avenue of Haywards Heath, which even back then featured two modern style pedestrian crossings.

This challenge was relatively easy to get away with in institutions such as the High Street banks and small supermarkets, but presented more of a contest in establishments like the carpet shop, where we would be approached with a weary "Can I help you?" Unenthused salespeople who I strongly suspect realised that my 13 year old self and my 11 year old sister weren't particularly interested in comparing pile and colour options across their particular range of fitted to order domestic bliss, and indeed didn't have the budget to carry our dreams through, would usher us out of the shop as quickly as they possibly could.

Unperturbed, we'd sweep east along the north side of the street before crossing over and returning west on the south side. This had the advantage of getting the carpet shop over and done with quite quickly, whilst saving the highlight (apart from the sweet shop of course) till near the end. At the western end of the teeming thoroughfare, just past the last pedestrian crossing, but before the buildings gave way to the town centre's immaculately landscaped park, was a record shop called Mastersound.

Mastersound became a crucial part of my teenage development. Later in life it became apparent to my schoolmates and myself that it was reachable within the lunch break, and we'd often forego school dinners to make the brisk walk there and back on release dates to purchase important singles. I remember two of us making this pilgrimage one day to purchase The Jam's "Going Underground" and returning to school proudly cherishing our copies much to the scorn of the heavy metal fans who had become our bitter rivals by that point. The sense of triumph felt when that record reached Number 1 in its first week of release lives with me to this day.

Mastersound was also the scene, in 1980, one Saturday morning, of local mod band The Lambrettas turning up and playing an impromptu set from the back of a pick-up truck parked outside the shop. The combination of this ultra-cool event and the bemused looks of the good people of the town going about their Saturday shopping was to become one of my defining moments as a teenager, when it began to feel like our time had come.

But back in the mid-70s Mastersound was no more than the most interesting of those shops up and down the street that had to be ticked off before we'd allow ourselves our weekly purchase of Tutti-Fruttis and sherbet lemons. It held some wonder for us, however, and we'd linger in there flicking through all the vinyl that we couldn't afford, listening to music being played, and overhearing conversations between customers and staff about the latest sounds and the developing musical world about which I was becoming so intensely curious.

After my musical epiphany in the second half of 1977 it became increasingly obvious that actually obtaining some of these records was going to be vital, so I got myself a paper round and started counting the pennies.

The number of mugs placed next to my parents' authentic 70s teas-made device before they retired to bed every night was increased to three, and my father would bring me in a cup of tea every morning at whatever early hour of the day it was that he rose to prepare for his daily commute. Quick as a flash I'd fall straight back to sleep again, stir again half an hour later, throw on some clothes, flush the now cold tea down the toilet so as to escape drawing attention to my tardiness and leave the house. I'd scurry down to the Haywards Heath station branch of WH Smith on my recently acquired pride and joy, a Halfords Olympic five-speed racing bike (funded entirely by my parents and several tokens lovingly separated from cereal packets which were themselves, of course, also funded by my parents).

The bike would be carefully placed into the shop's cycle rack, located on the seemingly endless ramp up to the platforms at the station, and temporarily replaced with whichever of the WH Smith owned bikes with built in bags for carrying newspapers looked the least like a death trap each particular morning. The bags would be filled with copies of the Daily Telegraph and The Times, interspersed with Daily Mails and Daily Expresses, an occasional Sun, and an even more occasional Guardian. Most days I'd quite enjoy my early morning exertions in the fresh air, and even when the weather was bad the knowledge that I was earning good, honest money that could subsequently be exchanged for circular pieces of plastic was more than enough to drive my ambition. Besides which, living in a house that didn't have a paper delivered itself, and where the only window to the world in the kitchen at breakfast time was Radio 4 news if I was lucky, having other people's papers to nose into before I slipped them through letter boxes gave me invaluable insights into what was happening in the real world, and most importantly what the previous night's football results had been.

Paper round completed, I'd return to the station to retrieve my bike, by which time countless hundreds of suit-clad Mr Cleans and Smithers-Joneses would be wending their way up to platforms 3 and 4 to be whisked off to London Bridge or Victoria. No doubt Woking was the inspiration for both of those mid-era Jam characters, but it could just as easily have been my hometown. Some days I'd see my father making his way to work, other days I'd see friends' dads, most days I seemed to see someone I knew. It seemed that most adult men in the town made this daily journey, and it also seemed to me to be somewhat tragic. I vowed to myself that I would never succumb to this way of earning a living.

Fortunately, of course, I wouldn't have to, because I was a punk, so obviously I was going to move to London anyway. I was not averse to the idea of working, after all I was already doing it and it was paying for my embryonic record collection, but I was never going to put myself in a position where I had to use up so much of my time travelling to or from somewhere to do it in some form of brain-numbing autopilot mode. Oh well, best laid plans and all that.

It is with great regret and not a little embarrassment that the first record that I actually walked into Mastersound and bought with my new-found disposable income was a minor Elton John hit from 1978. To this day I'm not sure why I selected this over any of the other records that were available at the time, but I know it was quickly followed into my burgeoning collection by Squeeze's "Take Me I'm Yours" and "She's So Modern" by The Boomtown Rats. I was probably just trying to reassure my parents that my hard-earned cash was being spent wisely, and by then my musical tastes had shifted so far from theirs that Elton John would have represented good, safe listening to their ears.

Every penny I earnt was spent on vinyl, exclusively singles at that stage as albums were out of my price range. I became friendly with the staff at Mastersound, who pretty soon were offering to play me things they thought I might like. As much as I owe to John Peel, I certainly have a debt of gratitude to a couple of the guys that worked in that sadly long defunct record shop. Without doubt they were responsible for introducing me to both The Ruts and The Lurkers and I am sure countless other bands as they emerged during that period.

My collection would be supplemented from any available channel. There was a shop at the other end of town that was fundamentally a convenience store but for some reason seemed to stock 7-inch singles that had recently left the chart at knockdown prices. I later acquired an original copy of "Another Girl, Another Planet" by The Only Ones from that late 70s bastion of the establishment, a Blue Peter "Bring and Buy Sale", for 5p. I wonder to this day who had decided to part with that particular classic as a charity donation, but no matter.

However, there was no substitute for the atmosphere of an actual record store. So one day when the schoolmate who had sold me that copy of "Tubular Bells" all those years ago suggested we visit a magical and mysterious place he described to me called Virgin Records in far-flung Brighton, I was enthralled. He explained that this place was like my beloved Mastersound, only five times the size, and you could go in and look at records all day long, and listen to some of them, and they had posters, and T-shirts, and all sorts of weird and interesting people could be found in there.

Despite the fact that I was now a fully mature nearly 14 years old streetwise Punk Rocker from Mid-Sussex, my parents warned me about travelling with a group of friends to Brighton. Although only a 22-minute train ride away I was cautioned as to how the town was a dangerous place, full of ne'er-do-wells, menaces and crooks who would rip us off at every opportunity. There were violent people there who would almost certainly attack us if they thought we were a "gang".

Leaving aside the fact that this Brighton was the same place as the town to which we had been dragged once a term since time immemorial to get kitted out in Marks and Spencer leisurewear, and that it hadn't seemed too scary on those occasions, I wasn't going to be perturbed. And anyway, as part of another of my lifelong hobbies I had been a regular train traveller to the County Cricket Ground with school friends since I was 12, and that had often involved walking through the badlands of Brighton Station's immediate environs if we couldn't get a direct train to Hove. It never seemed that dangerous to me. Therefore, I was going to go for it, and one Saturday morning we set off to the bright lights of Brighton's original Virgin Records store.

Wanna Do Something New

A decade before my own teenage musical expedition commenced, David Fenton was embarking on his own. Dave grew up in Redhill, an unremarkable town in Surrey, nestled just to the north of Gatwick Airport, some twenty miles nearer to London than Haywards Heath but otherwise probably fairly similar.

Dave's formative years, like my own, incorporated an early wide-eyed fascination with, and appreciation of, contemporary pop, but in his case that wonderfully treasure-strewn entity I had only discovered subsequent to its demise termed so evocatively by all and sundry as "The Sixties" provided his own personal backdrop. The absorption of music throughout that decade shaped his own life in a far greater, more participatory way than it had done my own. It led him to being not only as big a fan as I was, but much more impressively, to becoming a talented songwriter and music business professional, initially as a performer and subsequently as a lawyer.

One of the boundless truths about great music of any genre is its ability to be both timeless and completely date-specific in equal measures dependent on the mind of the beholder at any given point. I have no way of knowing, but I suspect that many inside the Royal Albert Hall in 1877 watching Richard Wagner conduct performances of his own music would have experienced emotional extremes not dissimilar to those that coursed through me a century later watching Jean-Jacques Burnel playing his own songs. To this day, millions of people around the globe treasure Wagner's music with almost religious fervour, yet none of them were around at the time of its creation. Who is to say whether that makes their immersion in that music any more or less intense than those who actually experienced it live in the controlling presence of its composer?

A century of rapid development in technology through transportation, electronics, broadcasting and more recently digital media has expedited that time lapse process in all facets of life, but for the music fan it can be starkly felt set against the equally rapid evolution of popular culture. During my early-70s musical awakening, Elvis Presley was just another name I associated with my BBC-driven musical education. I'd heard some of his recordings, but they didn't really do much for me, and in my young mind he was just another artist from ancient history who happened to be releasing new records sometimes. Ancient history is a subjective thing though, and there were people I would have known then, not much older than myself, who had been around when Elvis had hit the big time, who had experienced the excitement of his early career, perhaps who had seen him perform, and whose views would have been shaped for life as a result. And there are many who were born much, much later, who grew to love Elvis for the first-time long after his death, whose experience of his music may have been equally as heartfelt despite being in no way his contemporary.

Nevertheless, Pop Music has an ability to draw timelines very precisely because of its countless, ever changing, rapid metamorphoses. I have several close friends today, at similar points in their life journeys, with whom I share musical tastes and interests, but who happen to be just a handful of years younger than me. Some of them speak with genuine envy and even jealousy about how they never got to see certain bands in the late 70s that I did, simply because of that slight age difference. Indeed, my youngest son, now in his early twenties, has developed his own love for the same 90s music that I was listening to myself at the time, an era I have clear and happy memories of, and which doesn't feel like too long ago, even though in chronological terms, it is actually a time more distant from the present than Elvis' musical debut had been at the time I discovered music.

Dave Fenton's first rock concert experience perfectly illustrates the random incongruity between an age difference of a few years and the frequent, era-defining and line-drawing changes in popular music.

Dave's brother Derek, himself ten years Dave's senior, had his own turntable in the family home, and the records he would play on it began to seep into Dave's conscience at an early age. "What I heard from my brother was all I heard to start with," he recalls, continuing with a warm smile of reminiscence "I remember hearing late 50s and early 60s skiffle, Lonnie Donegan, that sort of thing, which is what The Beatles came in on."

Like our transistor fixated generation of a decade later, Dave began to tune in to the radio in his bedroom in the evening. "I'd listen to all sorts of shit on the radio, stuff from other different countries, all sorts, just to hear what was going on."

In 1963, at the age of just 10, the opportunity arose for that all important first gig. It was July and the family were in Bournemouth discussing what to do on one particular holiday day. "They asked me. It was me, pushing the rest of the family. My mum was there, my father was there, my younger brother was there. I said, 'we're not going to a funfair, can we go to this gig please?'" His parents agreed, and somewhat momentously, Dave got to see his first band. They were The Beatles.

He states, perhaps unsurprisingly albeit in a very matter of fact way that this was something of a life-changing event for him, as he recalls songs like "Love Me Do" being drowned out by the screaming, and the whole atmosphere and feel of the event being so, so much more than four blokes playing instruments and singing songs on a stage. "I think it was that one show," he surmises "on top of what I had heard from my brother and sought out on the radio, that if anything, was the thing that locked me into music."

He had been introduced to the spectacle of the live rock gig at a much earlier age than I was to be, and in some style, but Dave recalls the sense of anticipation and possibility that accompanied his formative musical educational journey through the decade with an enthusiasm and childlike wide-eyed smile with which I completely identify. He had the luxury of something that I never had, an older brother with a record collection, which informed his choice and steered his radio show hunting, and his own tastes developed accordingly. He lists bands from that era for whom I share his deep historical love, including The Small Faces, The

Kinks and The Stones, the difference being that these bands were his live childhood soundtrack, not something learned post-event. Who knows whether that changes the emotional perspective on how we both view those artists' work, and it takes nothing at all away from my permanently fond memories of the bands that dragged me into music in the early 70s in terms of how they steered me on my own journey from that point on. It's just that, set against the judgement of history, comparing Dave's Beatles, Kinks and Small Faces to my Sweet, Slade and Gary Glitter seems somewhat inspiring.

The fuse lit, he began to take the first steps into making his own music. He finds it difficult to remember the exact age at which listening transformed into participation, knowing only for sure that it was whilst still at school, having made friends with three others who were keen on playing together. "I learnt guitar from them, and they learnt guitar from me" he explains "and in the end we ended up with a 3-piece called 'Magician'."

Not having any income or any other form of spare cash to invest in amplifiers or drum kits, the band consisted of two acoustic guitars and a set of bongos, with two of its number sharing vocal duties. Perhaps due to the format of the band, whilst still at school they began to get bookings at local folk clubs. "We used to play all sorts of places, I remember The Greyhound in Croydon, we used to write tunes that we played on mandolin and all sorts of shit. We got places though, they'd let us stand up and play for 20 minutes," he remembers, adding wistfully "Blimey, that was 50 years ago." He points out, justifiably and proudly, that "the fact that we could take our places in an adult folk club and do what we were doing and be respected for it when we were school age was great."

All the while, Dave was receiving, and responding to, a successfully delivered and implemented education, despite his resentment of some of his tutors and advisors at school (and later sixth form college) who understood perfectly his achievement and potential, but nothing of his personality or of his aspirations for life. It was a frustration I was to feel myself in my own school environment, but like me Dave had supportive parents on board, albeit with a sense of expectation that he would translate early academic attainment into successful career building. Nonetheless, Dave recalls that his father, a headmaster, was never anything but supportive and encouraging whilst still offering solid, sound advice. He would later become very proud of his son's musical achievements as well as his academic ones.

Twenty miles west of Redhill, in Guildford, Steven Smith was born, a few years later than Dave. Steve freely admits that his academic potential was not as great as Dave's but nevertheless he is clearly an intelligent man. Details of his hometown schooling are patchy, and a number of web interviews and indeed Steve's own social media profiles refer simply and light-heartedly to the "School of Hard Knocks" when listing his educational background.

Nevertheless, Steve states often and in detail, with genuine satisfaction and passion in his voice, that once he had fallen in love with music, and began playing at an early age, energy was focused and targeted towards harbouring that skill. "I worked and worked, practised and practised" he enthuses, "and when I started playing in bands, we rehearsed and rehearsed, every available opportunity. We'd all do a day's work doing whatever we did every day, and then get together in the evening three, four, five times a week for band practice." It's a work ethic that still holds true to this day.

Steve's own musical tastes are hugely diverse and had been from an early age. This is perhaps reflected in the fact that, as the only member of The Vapors who maintained a full-time career on the performing side of the industry during the band's hiatus, the musical styles and diversity of the sounds that some of the bands he played within or was involved with span any number of genres. He cites "Anything I've ever listened to" as his musical influences and having listened to Steve on many occasions reeling off enthusiastically some of the songs and tunes he has loved over the years, it becomes obvious that the list is fairly long. Certainly, his post-original Vapors early 80s band Shoot! Dispute who attracted some moderate acclaim and success themselves, pushed away from the post-punk new wave formula and adopted the looser, pre-rave spiky, funkier sound that became part of the alternative end of the first half of that decade's musical development.

His first love, however, remains dirty noisy bass sounds, not unexpectedly, and he confesses to having more fun on stage playing with his punk-classic covers band The Shakespearos than with pretty much any outfit he has ever performed with.

Also in Guildford, and younger still than Steve, Ed Bazalgette and Howard Smith went through their secondary education together, meeting later during their school careers when they were introduced as a result of their musical connections, and becoming friends. Both being closer to myself in terms of age, it's perhaps unsurprising that their early tastes are the most similar to my own, with Howard citing The Clash as one of his early inspirations, both musically and, later in life politically, as he became active in local politics, still based in the town.

Ed lists a wide range of early memories and influences, but with a degree of commonality to my early 70s memories and later 70s awakening, cites Mott The Hoople, Simon and Garfunkel, The Jam, The Skids and The Specials amongst others, as well as the learned throwbacks towards whom we all seem to gravitate such as The Beatles, The Who and The Searchers.

At a similar time, far, far away from the Home Counties, in Jamaica, Michael Bowes was born. Michael's family moved to England when he was just four and a half, settling in Brixton. Perhaps unsurprisingly, Michael's earliest musical recollections are slightly different from mine, my peers, his future Vapors bandmates, and just about everyone else who appears in this book. "Reggae is ingrained in me, sure, subconsciously I guess. It was the only music I heard when I was very young" he explains. "But though I moved here before school I was kind of old enough to recognise the culture differences between Jamaica and London, but certainly reggae was still a big part of the background when we got to Brixton."

But genre specific or not, Michael just admits to "Being fascinated by drums and banging things. I used to sneak into my mum's kitchen when I was young and steal the tins of food, the actual tins of peas and tomatoes, and pots and saucepans and wooden spoons. I just needed to get all the different sounds out! It got me into trouble with her a few times but only caused me damage once when I ducked to avoid a flying tin when she finally snapped, and I banged my head on a doorknob!"

He recalls the Gospel Churches of South London where there would be bands and music, and most importantly, people banging things, and just decided from a really early age that he needed to play the drums. He remained frustrated at Primary School, where he was encouraged to sing and ended up performing acapella duets at school concerts with classmates, but his chance came as he moved up to Secondary School.

Now relocated to Croydon, where South London finally gives way to Surrey and the Home Counties, Michael was, in common with so many of us of a certain age, ready for Secondary School, but living in trepidation on account of some of the darker tales of what it would be like that were passed around by his 10-year-old classmates. "The school had a reputation, all those tales of bigger kids flushing your head down the toilet, that kind of thing," he says, "but I was persuaded to go there because I could learn drums. I got there and I was just the happiest kid because I was getting taught to play. At 11 and 12 it was just one drum, a single snare, but once older I got a whole drum kit to play on. It was just amazing, we had a great teacher, he just showed us all these different rhythms and I played and played."

But Michael had a parallel love, a fascination with aeroplanes, that would also serve him well in later life. "I had to wait till I was 13 to join the air cadets, and I was desperate to join the ones with the marching band, but I couldn't get into that one. So I joined 2157 Squadron in Mitcham, and just spent all of my teenage years doing that. And drumming really!"

Wide Eyes and Scruffy Hair

We set off on our group expedition to Brighton's Virgin Records store. Away from the grim, concrete hell of the 1970s form of the Churchill Square shopping centre, its direct neighbourhood of Western Road and the genteel seafront promenades of Hove and Rottingdean, the only areas of the conurbation I was thus far familiar with through family visits, the town (it wasn't a city back in those days) was everything I had hoped it would be.

We headed south from Brighton station. Virgin Records was indeed a new world of promise, but of much greater excitement was the area around the North Laine. These days this neighbourhood is a post-cool and tidy set of closely-knit streets that comprise a diverse set of slightly too trendy independent retailers, bars and cafes and which serves as a magnet for locals and tourists alike. In the mid-70s it was a much rougher (in the sense of being a bit down at heel, rather than dangerous) area, whose main retail offerings comprised of new and used clothes shops, and seemingly endless vinyl stores selling recent releases and second-hand records.

But these weren't the chart records of my world, or even the by now mainstream punk and new wave records that were supplementing my growing collection on a weekly basis. These places had an atmosphere of their own and were frequented by people who without exception would have stood out a mile during the daily morning suited exodus from Haywards Heath station. They smelt different, they looked different and, in many cases, they spoke different, often (I realised even then) as a result of the recent or not so recent absorption of any number of legally or illegally available substances that they may have obtained.

What I remember most about these people is their incredible kindness, and their general willingness to give us the time of day. I assume that they represented the type of individual that my parents had warned me about, but to a group of wide-eyed 13-year olds they were another fascinating addition to the increasingly magical and exponentially growing world of music that we were still learning was out there. The way they spoke to us in such a passionate, friendly and genuinely caring way about any of the records we spotted, the sounds we heard playing and the music scene in general, sparing us as much time as we wanted, conveyed a sense of warmth, wonder and excitement. We began, on this and several subsequent such trips, to reciprocate as we learnt over the years that as we were able to better interact socially with the world it would be something that would help to carry us through to adulthood.

I don't think any of us actually passed over any cash in any of those shops that day. But we spent the day moving from building to building, and street to street. We excitedly discussed each discovery, be it a record sleeve we liked the look of because of the design of its cover, or the look of the band photos, or the walls of the shops, or the songs we had been played in the shops, or the tall or otherwise stories we were told about legendary gigs that the characters we met may or may not have attended.

Ah yes. Gigs. The last link in the chain. Up until then, my experience of live music had been provided in its entirety by those endless performances featuring my parents when I was young, or more recently by being dressed up in shirt and tie to attend elite orchestral concerts in culturally-foreign (to me) locations like the Royal Festival Hall. I've stated already that these events never really enthused, and I knew by this stage that this was due simply to the fact that they comprised types of music that simply weren't quite to my taste. But that didn't mean that they didn't convey a sense of respect and amazement about the fact that a group of people could come together and make various noises with their voices and musical instruments, and that the sum of the parts could provide such an incredible sound.

I saw how much work my parents had put into their music, and to some extent how the more talented or hard-working amongst the constant flow of piano pupils stopping me from watching television after school applied themselves. As a consequence, I had a high level of admiration for anyone who was prepared to get up on stage and perform, even if the music they were producing wasn't exactly for me.

So what would it be like to actually go to a concert to see one of my newfound favourite bands perform themselves?

Fortunately, I didn't have long to wait, and in nothing but a positive way, it was a baptism of fire.

"Have you seen who's playing at the Brighton Centre next month?" asked my new posh black T-shirt wearing punk schoolmate from Dulwich one April morning. Somehow, I managed to persuade my parents that they should buy me a ticket as a birthday present. My friend's mother purchased them for us to complement the black T-shirts she had already provided (and that were now going to be worn for a real reason), and three days before I turned 14, I was off to see The Stranglers in concert.

Everyone remembers their first gig of course, and I'm lucky enough to have witnessed countless hundreds more special, special evenings in the years since. But here I was on May 20th, 1978 amongst a crowd of people, mostly (or maybe all) older than me, in various states of sobriety, some also wearing black T-shirts, many dressed even more exotically, and feeling like I was a part of something incredible.

I remember the bouncers dressed in snappy blue tracksuits and the undercurrent of violence that seemed to be bubbling through the hall without actually being threatening. Like the record shops of the North Laine, this place had a smell of its own comprising alcohol, sweat, tobacco and other forms of smoke-related products. I remember the support band, fronted by Brian James who had recently left The Damned, and how they were booed and jeered throughout their set in what I realised even at the time was all part of the ritual.

But most of all I recall the moment when Jean-Jacques, Hugh, Dave and Jet, less than a year after waking up my life with that "Top Of The Pops" performance, swaggered on stage, picked up their instruments and produced 90 minutes of immense, glorious noise. I couldn't have kept still even if I had wanted to as I bounced my legs up and down in the safety of my balcony seat.

The volume, the noise of that bass, the atmosphere generated by the crowd, the lights, all surpassed expectations and I didn't want the evening to end. The "Black and White" album had just been released and the single "Nice 'n' Sleazy" was performed with the added assistance of a stripper. A lot has been written over the years about The Stranglers and their lack of political correctness, or worse still their (perceived or otherwise) misogyny during this period, however to a boy just about to turn 14 that wasn't uppermost in my mind. I had never seen anything like it. Literally.

Before I knew it, Hugh had unstrapped his guitar, slung it down whilst the rest of the band finished the song and left the stage, and I was shortly introduced to the ceremony of the rock gig encore.

Quick as a flash it was over. My father picked us up from outside the Brighton Centre with our ears ringing and the adrenaline pumping. The late-night wild streets of Brighton still meant unlimited menace and danger in the eyes of my parents, but of course the ease and safety of a lift home was secretly very welcome.

That completed the circle. My lifetime as a fully-fledged music fan was officially up and running.

Many people, especially of course from my generation, recall at length their experiences of the music scene in the late 1970s. The time, and the era, was a special one. The records, the gigs, the clothes, the culture, and most of all the music itself, set against the social and economic background of the period, represent a five-year passage that in many ways was like no other in British history. Regular conversations with friends, acquaintances and strangers I meet for the first time either in person or online to this day continue to inform me as to how widespread and diverse this passion runs across a large swathe of my generation.

We all have our own natural favourite memories, some strong, some less so, some clearly remembered, and others blurred in the mists of time. But there is one experience, one recollection, that repeatedly seems to burn brighter, and draw more unsolicited enthusiasm amongst those that were there than any other from that time, and that is the memory of witnessing The Jam playing live. Almost universally, anyone who ever got to see this band perform seems to adopt an excited, quickening of the heart narrative when they catalogue their own reminiscences of their shows. The sense of awe-struck anticipation that charged the atmosphere before these gigs, the raw energy that coursed through the crowd during the performances, and the sheer venom, anger, fire and skill (to borrow a phrase) with which the songs were delivered by the band was, and remains in my mind, unique. Even in the band's latter years, when the songs and musical arrangements gained complexity and subtlety, and the concert halls gave way to arenas, the electric intensity of the shows never lessened.

I was lucky enough to see The Jam many times, and the rose-tinted spectacles have never lost their sharpness when they focus back through time and revisit the nights. This was a special band. They had been around for a while when I first got to see them, late on in 1978, whilst they were touring the "All Mod Cons" album, at the Brighton Dome. I was still in my gig infancy at this point, and still electing to acquire tickets nestled within the safety of the balcony seats, but this time I had travelled to the gig with my black T-shirt friend and a couple of other schoolmates who were beginning to share our interest in the contemporary music scene.

We took our seats, allowed ourselves to be amused by the US humour-punk of support band The Dickies, and awaited the arrival of the headliners. In those days, the Dome was a completely seated venue, and we scrutinised the Stalls from our lofty position upstairs, all of us coming to the realisation that we'd much rather be amongst the regulation-dressed Punk Rockers (the mod explosion was only just being ignited at that point) who were incongruously spread amongst the grand theatre-style rows of seats below. As the house lights dimmed, we gazed in wonder as the seated lethargy gave way in a split second to a collective dash of bodies to the front of the stage, rendering vast swathes of the auditorium unpopulated. One of our number yelled "Come On!" and in a whirl the four of us leapt down the stairs, somehow keeping our footing as we ran uncontrollably and unchecked like dizzy toddlers through the doors into the downstairs section, and joined the burgeoning throng in front of the stage, just as John Weller took to the microphone to announce the arrival of his son's band.

Suddenly we were a part of it. Watching The Stranglers six months previously had been special, as had been watching the behaviour of their audience, and as it had been at all of the gigs I'd been to in the interim period. But now, we were in the crowd. We were amongst the sweaty, heaving mass of excitement, and we were a contributory part, no longer onlookers. As the band played, we leapt, pogoed, shouted, pumped fists and let the adrenaline control us whilst the music and the noise carried us. Gigs would never be the same again, partly because we now knew how to join in, but partly because even then, at the first of my many Jam gigs, there was an innate sense that I had been a part of something truly unique.

Throughout my formative years my friendships had been varied and largely transient. Friends came and went, some of whom had influences on my early years' musical tastes as already described, others who had influences on the other great love of my childhood years, namely sport, and others who just came and went.

I was acquainted with a boy called Kevin from the beginning of secondary school, but at the age of thirteen or so, whilst The Stranglers were contributing increasingly to the shaping of my teenage years, Kevin and myself began to find other interests in common and began to spend time together at school and on the way home afterwards discussing varied topics. Music (of course), football (his taste in teams remains misguided to this day but that didn't cause a problem), Motor Racing (of which he was an aficionado, and about which I was developing an interest as a result of his enthusiasm), bikes, girls, all the usual teenage boy stuff really, were discussed at length over and over again.

Kevin introduced me to the mysterious, eerie sound of Radio Luxembourg which formed an alternative access method to the exciting new musical sounds I was discovering at pace at the time, and in turn Radio Luxembourg introduced me to the New Musical Express through the medium of radio advertising

It was to be slightly over a year before I saw The Jam again, at The Brighton Centre, in December 1979. I was still only fifteen, but the year since the Dome gig had seen me grow up in many ways, none more significantly than regular gig-going becoming a major part of my social outlook. I had become appreciably better informed about the whole of the music scene both locally (in Brighton) through experience, and further afield through weekly blanket reading of the music press. NME was not enough on its own anymore, most weeks Sounds, Melody Maker and Record Mirror were somehow also acquired and scanned end to end as I pieced together in my head the connections across time and cultures that I was running so hard to get up to speed with.

My friendship with the posh Dulwich punk fizzled out, largely due to him selling his soul to the devil and becoming interested in Heavy Metal. However, my friendship with Kev blossomed and grew, and by the time that the next Jam tour came around had cemented into the lifelong bond that still exists today. Amongst our other interests, music had begun to provide us more and more common ground. Unlike me, Kev had inherited some of his parents' own musical tastes, but then unlike my parents, Kev's mum and dad were both into rock and pop. Kev tried (and failed) to interest me in some bands towards the Prog side of the rock spectrum, but he also had an early love for The Who's back catalogue that he persuaded me with ease to share, and we would listen to a lot of their music together, using both records plundered from his parents' collection, and ones that he had acquired himself. Throughout the year I had reciprocated by playing Kev selections from my now fast expanding punk and new wave singles and albums collection and, amongst others, his admiration for, and appreciation of, The Jam's "All Mod Cons" album quickly grew to match my own. We began to go to gigs together, and at the same time developed our first fledgling interest in fashion, in a stereotypical Fred Perry shirt and Harrington Jacket kind of way. The black T-shirt gave way to something a little more sophisticated, as everything came together musically and socially and we found ourselves part of, and absolutely loving being a part of, the late 70s mod revival.

"Setting Sons" was released, and I played it to Kev who listened wide-eyed, whilst still not knowing an awful lot about The Jam. "Has this guy ever written a rock opera?" he asked in all innocence as "Little Boy Soldiers" echoed from the stoic gramophone unit and he made the mental connection between Townsend and Weller for himself that was being made all over the rest of the music world at the time. I remember laughing and saying something about how rock operas probably didn't quite fit the punk ideal, but we both instinctively knew that we were listening to something extraordinary, and like many others I hold that album dear to this day, one of a small handful of untouchables that represent that era irrevocably.

Fairly obviously, we would need to get to see The Jam together at the next available opportunity, and that winter's tour, arranged to coincide with the release of the album, gave us the opportunity. Gig tickets for the more popular bands were as hard to come by then as they are now, but the methods of obtaining them were less sophisticated. NME would announce the tour dates, we'd ring the venue to check for "on sale" times, and many an early morning would be spent in drizzly concrete queues outside places like the Brighton Centre, the Hammersmith Odeon and the late, lamented Rainbow Theatre in Finsbury Park to ensure ticket acquisition. The arrangement for The Jam's "Setting Sons" tour was no different, so one autumnal morning we jumped on the first train to Brighton and at approximately 6.30am joined what was already a long queue of people waiting for the 10.00am opening of the Brighton Centre's ticket office. The black leather heavy punk uniform of my previous Jam experience had given way to parkas and Harrington Jackets, tatty torn jeans replaced by smart crisp trousers, but this time I wasn't an outsider joining in. I felt like I belonged, and I was firmly a part of it. Even queuing for tickets in the rain at stupid o'clock on a windswept Brighton seafront for a gig that was weeks away carried that sense of anticipation that only The Jam could engender.

On the night of the gig, we arrived at the venue about an hour before the doors even opened, as we always did back then, where the pre-Jam gig excitement level was already high. We had standing tickets and we'd be rushing straight to take our places at the front the minute we were allowed in, which had become the norm but often involved having to stand through one or more dull support acts just to maintain our places for the main event. Not all support bands were dull of course, and we were optimistic on this particular occasion. The opening act for the whole of the tour were a band that had attracted some positive press during the lead-up period, whose name we had seen splashed across the myriad Live Ad pages for most of the year, and who were a band who seemed to be gaining a fairly solid reputation. That band was called The Vapors.

For a group who were to become so central to the next few years of my music fan's life, and who were to return to it so spectacularly in the distant future, my introduction to the music of The Vapors was relatively low key. I certainly remember enjoying their performance but set against the buzz of the rising anticipation of the imminent arrival of the headline act it was, in every sense of the word, a supporting role that my soon to be new favourite band played that night. I remember that they were competent, I remember that there were some good tunes, and rather inevitably I remember the song that stood out, a pop song slightly quirkier than the others, with a stick-in-the-mind chorus, named "Turning Japanese".

Given that the band played so many gigs in quick succession the length and breadth of the country, it is not surprising that, forty years on, none of them can recall too much about the detail of many of them. Steve does remember the Brighton show with a laugh, however. "We only ever played 'Here Comes The Judge' as an encore on that tour, and we only got an encore about five times." Leaving aside the fact that this is no mean feat for a support act on a major tour, he continues "We went on stage and completely fucked it up! Only thing I remember about the night! Everyone got lost. It was that thing where you want the floor to open up. It was horrific. Normally one of us might lose it a bit, that night we all did."

I'm not sure that either Kev or I had detected any fault in the performance, but they were on our radar. The talk at school the next day was not just about the inevitable brilliance of The Jam, but also about the support band, for whom Kev and I agreed between us we'd be keeping an eye out in future.

During 1979, in the months leading up to that December Jam concert, gig going had burst through the boundaries of the upstairs seats at the two large Brighton venues we'd first inhabited in 1978. The humble button badge had become ubiquitous and essential. Proudly sporting badges acquired either at gigs or via mail order from Better Badges, a regular advertiser in the NME whose name will be remembered with unfettered fondness by all music fans of a certain age and demographic, I was now able to advertise my musical allegiances on my school blazer, all day long. Through this simple medium I connected with other like-minded individuals, some in my own year group, others in older year groups, and they in turn shared their knowledge and opinions. Via my new friends' older siblings, I became aware of the vibrant music scene unfolding in my own backyard in Brighton, and I tagged along with older kids to gigs featuring The Piranhas, Nicky And The Dots, and a band featuring one of the said older kids' mates on guitar, The Chefs, amongst many others.

Most of these gigs were in pubs, where the age restriction rules were murky to say the least, but I was never refused entry to any of the venues that Brightonian music fans of the day will recall with a nostalgic tear. Places like The Basement Club, The Richmond (recently reborn in a much-needed reversal of the current tide of venue closures) and the legendary Alhambra, a long-demolished seafront pub separated from the beach by the dual-carriageway tarmac of Kings Road in the days before urban traffic management all became regular destinations. With its stage set up in the bay window and a downstairs club that could be accessed by gig goers I spent more Sunday evenings at The Alhambra during my sixteenth year than I spent with my family eating Sunday roasts.

We'd still venture out to the big venues to see the big bands (and I would always do so, and indeed still do), but the horizon was a hundred times broader. We'd rehearse over and over again our fictitious dates of birth so as to be convincing when challenged upon entry to the Top Rank Suite, also on Brighton seafront, and the only place where the door policy was very clearly publicised as over eighteens only. No matter, we always got in without any trouble there too. The Top Rank Suite at that time was a regular stopping point for bands on the up who were playing breakthrough tours, and promoters would often pack the bill with tour support bands as well as local bands, resulting in sweaty gigs in a wonderful all standing venue that lasted for hours, and frequently caused issues with the thorny problem of whose dad we should ring to beg for a lift home hours after the last train had left Brighton. The Members played the venue in May of 1979, just before my fifteenth birthday, almost exactly a year since that first Stranglers experience around the corner, supported by two local favourites of the time, The Piranhas as well as Nicky And The Dots. I remember thinking that night how long ago The Stranglers gig had seemed, and how much had changed for me in that time.

So as 1979 drew to a close, the logical next step for Kev and me was to cast our nets a little wider. All of the music papers had large gig advert sections, and another treasured memory for many from that age will be the "NME Gig Guide" and equally, the prominent full page of adverts opposite it placed there by venues advertising the following week's shows. Top left of this page was always a stark list of acts topped with the logo of The Marquee, a club whose name evoked feelings of excitement and possibility to us long before we had ever set foot in the place. We were aware of its history, both distant and recent, but we were also aware of its promise through the constant stream of gig reviews that seemed to appear following appearance after appearance there by bands that were very much a part of our teenage years.

Just before Christmas we decided upon a last-minute shopping trip to London, agreeing that we'd use the day out to take in a gig at whatever venue we could find that had something on that we might like. We scoured the NME and discovered that The Pretenders were playing The Marquee on Saturday 22nd December. That fitted the bill.

Despite our now regular trips to Brighton, and late nights in the town's pubs and clubs, a trip to London still felt like an adventure. Visits to the capital up until then had largely been confined to family outings to museums or classical concerts, but the London we were intending to head to that day was the one we'd read about, mostly, if not entirely, informed by the journalistic content of the NME. We caught the train to Victoria, where we armed ourselves with one-day Travelcards and headed off on a tube-bound adventure taking in any area where we were vaguely aware that there were shops, and where we therefore assumed there would be records to buy. We headed to Oxford Street, then to Kensington High Street, then back to Oxford Street. It would take years to discover all that London had to offer of course (if anyone ever does) but the freedom of unlimited tube travel was exhilarating. We travelled to Bank, because we liked the name, stuck our heads out at the top of the stairs, observed the deserted Saturday City streets and retreated back down the escalator immediately. We traversed a bit of the Circle Line, and then re-traversed our way back, finally reaching Oxford Street for the third and final time that day before hitting McDonald's and consulting the A-Z we'd bought earlier to help us locate Wardour Street.

We arrived at The Marquee and paid our entrance fee. "How old are you?" we were asked brusquely. "Eighteen" we both spluttered unconvincingly. "You don't look it" came the matter of fact reply from the bored looking woman in the ticket booth, "and anyway, you don't have to be eighteen to get in." "Well that's alright then isn't it?" I offered. "No," she droned on "because if you're not eighteen, you can't buy alcohol." Realising that we couldn't lose face, but displaying early diplomatic skills, we persisted with the argument that we were eighteen, but agreed that we wouldn't buy alcohol, and she pressed a button that released two bus-style tickets from the metal dispenser built into the counter. Kev and I made mental notes to fine-tune our age-convincing strategy in future, but we were in, and we were walking down the narrow, subterranean, red and black passage that opened up into the tiny Marquee bar, through which we walked into the dark, cramped space that was to become such a special, special place to us in the years to come, and that had been loved by so many others before us.

Torn between the need to adopt our now de facto gig position at the front of the stage and the need to protect the vinyl treasures we'd purchased on our tortuous trek around Central London's mainstream shopping thoroughfares, we settled for a spot by the wall to the left of the room. We nestled under the glass DJ box where legendary names from those NME adverts resided providing the pre, mid and post gig soundtracks for so many shows.

We caught The Pretenders at the right time, there was a certain buzz around the band at that moment, and a few weeks later they would be at number one with "Brass In Pocket". I'd never label them as one of my favourite bands and taken within the context of the musical performance itself, I certainly wouldn't list the night as anywhere near my list of favourite gigs. But that wasn't the point. We'd been to a gig at The Marquee. We knew how to do it, we understood the process, and we'd connected the world of the pages in the music papers to the real world of the London music scene, and we weren't going to look back.

We both agreed that we needed to return to London, and more specifically to The Marquee as soon as possible, only this time we would need to see one of "our" bands, not just a band that we'd plucked from the paper because they happened to be on the night we would be in town. We loved the whole feel of small venue gigs which had been engendered in us earlier that year on the South Coast, but which felt more edgy, more authentic and which of course we already knew existed on a much grander scale in London. We needed a band who could truly excite us musically, who played regularly in London, whose gigs we could experience close up in dark, boozy, sweaty venues with like-minded human beings, and that didn't require weeks of planning to see, or queuing up outside ticket offices at the crack of dawn to gain entry to.

Christmas, New Year, January and mock "O" Levels came and went, and the weekly scouring of the NME live ads continued unabated. The opportunity we were waiting for came along shortly without too much ado. The 17th of February 1980 would feature a London gig, at The Marquee, performed by the band we'd seen supporting The Jam a couple of months previously, and who definitely fitted the bill in terms of the type of music we wanted to experience in that venue. We decided we'd travel up to town one late winter Sunday night to see The Vapors.

Go Johnny Go

Other than what we'd read in the music press, the Jam support set that we'd witnessed, and the fact that we were loving the by now released "Turning Japanese" single in the excited, can't-get-enough manner that music fans do, we knew very little about the band.

Following his early forays into live performance whilst still at school, Dave had passed his "A" levels and obtained a place at Nottingham University, where he read law from 1971 to 1974, whilst becoming a regular gig-goer in his own right, recalling in particular early 70s staples such as Mungo Jerry and Golden Earring.

Whilst there, Dave immersed himself in music as best he could, helping put on bands and shows in student union bars, whilst studying diligently. A crack at the music world was always in mind, but "Get the bits of paper first, then my parents can't argue" was the mantra, "then I can take a year off later and try the music thing."

Qualifying in law is a long and tortuous process, and involves not only the initial undergraduate training, but the gaining of experience in practice, and further subsequent training, before the end result is finally achieved. Following his time in Nottingham, Dave moved back down to Surrey and took up a position with a firm in Guildford. Post degree, and living back with his parents, he'd drive to Guildford and back every day before eventually selling the car and moving into a flat closer to work, using the proceeds from the car sale to fund the purchase of his first ever amplifier.

By this point, his thoughts had turned to setting up on his own in the music world. He'd got the bits of paper, had the insurance of having the requisite foundations for successful career building in the future, and quit the job, giving himself a year to make some headway.

"One day I was dealing with someone's divorce, I remember that specifically," he giggles, "and the next time I saw the woman I was selling her potatoes in a greengrocer's which was my way of paying the rent whilst I tried to get the music going."

Punk was underway, with the music scene in Guildford being as vibrant as it was anywhere else outside of the big cities, and Dave genuinely recalls the feel of the time. "Anyone can do this. Get up on stage and see what you can do. Everyone was interested." Feeding off that energy, Dave accelerated his search for bandmates, and armed with electric guitar for the first time, and swept along with the times and his later influences, the songs became a little pacier and noisier. "I wasn't thrashy, I had tunes. But the move was to fast rock songs rather than acoustic ones, influenced by the times. I just did what I liked."

He recollects an evening at The Marquee, already a regular part of his own gig-going voyage, where he went to see a favourite of his at the time, a long-lost band called The Screeens. "I can't remember if they were supporting or the main band that night," he says "but that wasn't the thing really. I'd been to see them at my brother's college down in Chichester. I thought they were brilliant. The front man was inspirational, I just wanted to be like him."

But as well as the band he'd gone to see, what really inspired Dave that night at The Marquee was the house DJ playing Devo between the sets. "'Jocko Homo' it was, and I was transfixed. I'd never heard anything like that, it wasn't even in 4/4 time" he adds bringing a touch of detail befitting the analysis of a musician. "I sought out their records and they became a lifetime favourite."

I've never had the heart to tell Dave that, impressive as I find his performances, I've never quite seen any Devo in his stage presence, but I guess that's missing the point. Branka points only to one occasion she can recall, when the reformed American art-rockers and electro-pioneers played at the Meltdown Festival at The Royal Festival Hall in 2007, and she reminds Dave fondly but in the unmistakable teasing tone of an amused wife that "You were down the front, doing some sort of berserk robot dance all bloody night long."

Spark now truly ignited, in 1978 Dave assembled bandmates and refined the set of songs that he was currently working with, explaining their evolution into what became The Vapors' initial repertoire simply. "When I did get a band together, and it fell apart a few times to start with, the songs just seemed to work, and we trimmed them right down."

The mark 1 version of the band, with Rob Kemp on lead guitar, Mike Jordan on drums and Mike Hedges on bass taking the stage alongside Dave, played their first ever gig at Lakers Hotel (now a Toby Carvery) near Redhill station, getting changed before the show at his parents' house just down the road.

In one of those "Hold on, what did you just say?!" moments, Dave recalls almost in passing that his support band that night was a three-piece (at the time) from down the road called The Cure. When pushed about this he'll say, "Yeah it's funny isn't it, we should have been supporting them really I think." He also recalls how the whirlwind events of the eighteen months that were to follow were encapsulated when he next bumped into Robert Smith in a hotel in Melbourne. "We'd got there, and they'd got there. I was from Redhill, they were from Crawley and Horley, that made it a very small world to me."

Throughout the year, more gigs were played, in both Surrey and London, band members came and went, and by the end of that winter the final line-up was settled. "Three or four bands broke down at the same time, so I just went around choosing bandmates" Dave explains, making it sound as easy as a trip to Woolworth's for some pick'n'mix. "I was on my own schedule, and it just fell into place." The youngest of the band members, Edward Bazalgette, fresh from recently split local band Ellery Bop, was the first to join, on lead guitar.

After leaving school Steve Smith had immersed himself in every aspect of the music scene in his own backyard and further across Surrey and London. He became friendly with a couple of guys who ran a small PA company. "I was already a musician, I'd played in a band since I left school, we played the circuit a bit." By 1978 his PA mates were beginning to do some work with Dave Fenton's mark 1 Vapors, and asked Steve along to help one night. "I ended up helping with The Vapors' PA at gigs, and began fiddling with sound too," he explains, continuing "I actually did the sound for them at the Music Machine gig the first line-up played, I think that was the only London gig they played."

In common with many of us to follow, he states simply "I just thought they were brilliant. Dave's songs were excellent."

As the year wore on, and the band's name became known around the Guildford area, rumours spread around the closely-knit town's music community that the bassist might leave to head off to University. "Simple," thought Steve, "I want this job." He spoke to Dave, arranged a demo, and was hired.

"The very next day the drummer, Mike Jordan, left the band. I thought 'blimey, what did I do?'" Steve doesn't recall seeing his former bandmate of just one day ever again, right up until he came to a reformed Vapors show in 2017. "It had taken nearly 40 years," he smirks, "but I finally got to ask him, was I that shit at the audition that you couldn't take any more?"

Two new drummers were on the radar, and the final piece of the jigsaw was slotted into place when Howard Smith auditioned and got the job, and off they went. "We slogged and slogged," continues Steve "and in turn the band worked. It just took off, we were feeding off each other, and Dave would be coming in each time we practised with a brilliant new song for us to work on."

Almost immediately, the band played together for the first time to a public (of sorts) audience during the lunch break at Godalming College, and then on the 11th of January 1979 played their first music venue gig, one of several to follow at The Three Lions in Farncombe. Situated just south of Guildford, the pub hosted a music club known as "Scratchers" which, unlike so many other venues of the time, still exists and thrives in the same capacity and with the same name today.

For sure Dave, and indeed the others, had served some form of their own musical apprenticeships, although Dave's was sandwiched around his legal training, but the remainder of 1979 constituted a tumultuous rise in status that most bands would be hard pushed to emulate.

A further gig at Scratchers one Sunday during the early spring was the catalyst, being the well documented occasion when The Jam's Bruce Foxton happened to walk into the pub and see them perform, immediately offering them a support slot on a couple of dates on his band's upcoming UK tour.

In May, third on the bill, The Vapors opened up for The Jam at notable rock circuit venues, Bristol's Colston Hall and Portsmouth's Guildhall. At the latter, they were called back for an encore by the crowd, a not inconsiderable achievement for a band playing first on the bill in the context of only their second ever gig as the second support act to a major band. The pace that their rapid ascent was gathering was not lost on them. "I remember getting picked up from work, soundcheck, straight on stage." Steve remembers of the first Jam support slot. "It was mad, never done anything like that."

Suitably impressed, John Weller took note, and in partnership with Bruce the pair offered the band a management contract. Although a popular and fanatically followed successful live and chart act by that point, The Jam had yet to quite ascend to the superstardom level that was to follow with number one singles and tours of the largest arenas. Dave offers the opinion that, certainly in Bruce's case, he may have been looking for other opportunities to diversify his skill set based upon the openings that his own grafting with his band on their rise had in turn afforded him, making managing an up and coming act an interesting side project.

Not long after, of course, The Jam did indeed hit the very big time, and ultimately Weller and Foxton had to abandon their managerial project, but not before the association, coupled undoubtedly with the fact that The Vapors had a significant talent and uniqueness of their own, had led to a record deal being signed with United Artists.

"It was crazy," smiles Dave "we'd only just got playing really, Ed and Howard had just finished their 'A' levels, and by September we had a record deal," before adding with a wider grin "yeah, a deal before my parents started moaning."

Discussions about the release of recorded material followed, the seemingly obvious use of "Turning Japanese" as a single was discussed, but it was decided to hold the song back until the band had been publicised and become a little better known. As a result, Dave wrote, specifically with the intention of using it as the first single, and the band recorded, "Prisoners" which was released at the end of October. Recording of the first album began soon after, as did The Jam's landmark "Setting Sons" tour, with The Vapors second on the bill on each of the shows on the near thirty-date round Britain trip.

Live At The Marquee

The 17th of February came around. The venue was exactly the same as we remembered from a couple of months previously (and which remained the same forever until its sad and still mourned demise). This time there was no questioning of our age as we entered, and buoyed by the certain knowledge that this must have meant that we looked like we were eighteen, we headed straight to the bar and bought ourselves pints of lager.

We'd arrived early but the place was heaving. We were well aware through our wall to wall weekly blanket scouring of the music media that the post-Jam tour buzz around the band had evolved into full-on hype, and furthermore the previous week "Turning Japanese" had been released as the band's second single.

Steve Smith describes the gig in very simple terms. "It felt like the whole of fucking Guildford was there" he recalls, and whilst Kev and myself were aware that the entire audience were on board, supportive and knew every word of every song, we didn't necessarily connect at first with the fact that this was a triumphant coming-of-age show performed by a band about to hit the big time, however briefly. The audience was comprised of a significant number of the band's music industry backers, a significant number of their journalistic supporters, and most importantly a significant number of their overtly, and justifiably, fiercely proud friends and hometown supporters.

Despite our new-found but still savagely underfunded attention to current fashion trends, and our unswerving loyalty to our new mod world, we didn't really object to the fact that most of the people there were dressed in a way that can only be described as pretty normal, despite the fact that by now, due mainly to The Jam connection, The Vapors had been lazily labelled as a "mod band". Sure, there were some mod uniform wannabees, as well as some late-punk homages, the occasional "look at me" stick-of-rock trousers and the odd spiky hair/big hair morphing prototype, but by and large it was a jeans and t-shirt wearing bunch of mainly young, mainly (but not overwhelmingly) male, normal, friendly folk.

Maybe because we were slightly more relaxed than we had been at previous gigs, maybe because we were just that slightly bit more mature, or maybe because this was a genuinely slightly different subset of the population to that which we had encountered at other gigs, we began to chat unreservedly to others, who seemed just as willing to reciprocate. The usual subjects were covered of course; music, football and the political situation which as we raced towards sixteen we were becoming increasingly aware of and increasingly concerned about. But the overall feeling of the night was one that has carried through each and every one of the band's shows that I have ever attended since, both then and now, one of camaraderie and respect. For ones still very much in our formative years, this was a powerful feeling that was to fuel and drive our obsession with this particular group in the coming months.

Opening up that night was a band called UBz, who we knew nothing about, but who we'd learnt from our conversations already that evening also hailed from the Guildford area, had been around The Vapors for a while, and who also seemed to have most of the friends they could ever have mustered in their lifetimes up until that point in the audience.

We barged our way to our now customary gig positions at the front of the stage prior to the arrival of UBz, last pennies spent on as much beer as that week's paper deliveries had allowed, staking out our places for the arrival of the main men, but happy to enjoy what a large number of the audience were clearly anticipating first. A boisterous leap around the stage by a youthful mate of Steve's, still a friend today, named Dylan Cole and his bandmates followed.

Dylan won't thank me for pointing out that I remember nothing of his music, but his boundless energy, enthusiasm and somewhat (then, as now) eccentric demeanour stayed in my head throughout life after this performance (and one or two others that year). Our paths re-crossed in early 2019, when we met in the back of a minibus enroute to a Vapors gig in faraway Minehead during which he entertained the assembled band members and family for the duration of the journey there and back again with any number of tall tales and anecdotes.

Back at The Marquee, UBz played their set and were dutifully but appreciatively acknowledged by the crowd for doing so. Kev and I joined the cheers and applause, swept along by the feelgood expectation by now coursing through the club, and held our places firm as we waited for the evening's star turns to arrive on stage.

In terms of what followed that year and through in to 1981, we were still on an upward curve with this band, and it would be a few months yet before their permanent etching in our hearts was completed. At this point we knew only of "Turning Japanese" which we remembered from that Jam gig, and which we had both already bought at Mastersound upon its release day, and its B-side. As we heard some of the other songs that night, however, there was some glimmer of familiarity triggered in our heads stemming from the only previous occasion we had seen them performed. This time, set amongst the context of an audience who were there specifically to see them, rather than the band they were supporting, we were able to identify and latch on more immediately to specific songs that still echo through my head most days even in my mid-fifties.

"This one's about hanging about on railway stations" announced Dave, or Steve, or Ed, for the first of many, many times in our presence, and the cheer that went up from the crowd instantly informed us that "Trains" was clearly a favourite of those in the know, to whom we quickly added ourselves. "America" sticks in the mind from that night, as does "Prisoners" (which we both hurriedly went out and purchased the following weekend once we'd become aware that there was such a thing as another Vapors record for us to acquire). Encore "Here Comes The Judge" was the only other song we were already really aware of due to its appearance on the B-side of "Turning Japanese" but we were already developing a familiarity with Dave Fenton's slightly different, but painfully tuneful and addictive songs, and the live musical delivery of them by The Vapors.

More importantly, that evening we had been a part of something that not only had we felt in some way that we were contributors to, as we had already felt at that Jam gig, but that was set amongst a bunch of kindred, sociable, non-threatening peers, with whom we had forged friendships just by, well, talking to people around us.

We had found our band.

We observed, with a time-frozen amazement, as "Turning Japanese" climbed the charts that spring, championed by numerous Radio 1 DJs, most memorably in Dave's recollection Dave Lee Travis who "seemed to play it on his show every day. I nearly fell out of bed one morning when my radio alarm clock switched on and I was woken up by my own bloody song." Our newly adopted favourite band appeared on "Top Of The Pops", which still held a fascination for me as the place where I had first been delivered my musical interest and knowledge. Before we knew it or were able to boast about it to our disinterested associates at school, the song was number three in the UK charts, and had entered the Billboard top forty in the US. It was everywhere, and the band were on an upward spiral that we had seen with other bands before, but which this time felt quite personal, and in a strange way rewarding to us, because of our determined affiliation to the group.

Like most Vapors fans I am sure, I have spent most of my life explaining to anyone who cares to listen, banging on and on about my obsession with this band whilst qualifying for their benefit that "you may not remember their name, but you'll remember their big hit single." I will then patiently explain that there were actually two high quality albums' worth of material that, in my opinion, and that of many others too, contain many songs that are far superior to the three minutes for which they are remembered around the world. They are almost as well known for the conjecture as to the rumoured salacious meaning of the song that stems from a typical Dave Fenton answer to a question in an American interview of the time, when he was asked to confirm, or deny, the by then popular explanation. Pretty much any time I, or any of my contemporaries ask Dave what any particular song is actually about, he will give his stock answer which is along the lines of "If that's what you want it to be about, sure." When this response was delivered to the American interviewer's specific question, therefore, it was widely interpreted as meaning "Yes" even though it probably wasn't. The reality is, however, that the band are eternally grateful, feeling that the public debate that followed can only really have led to increased volumes of sales.

I've always resisted the temptation to ask Dave to clarify for once and for all what he had in mind when he wrote the song, reasoning that he'd be very unlikely to tell me, and that actually, he does genuinely feel that all of his songs were written in such a way that people are very welcome, encouraged even, to apply their own interpretation. I have, however, spoken with him about another obvious question that is often asked in relation to the band's mega-hit, namely that of whether it ultimately became a millstone for them. Naturally, the song still gets an airing at every gig the band play and is of course always enthusiastically received. However, it is generally tucked away a few songs before the end of the set, as the beginning of the crescendo to the finale, rather than the show's climax itself, and at a recent festival appearance Dave even introduced it as "This is the one we don't like playing." I challenged him about this and he grinned back a dismissive "Oh I always say something flippant", but in reality he says it would be completely impossible for any songwriter not to love a composition of their own that is recognised the world over, that the band perform regularly, and that is known and sung along to by all present at every show. "But I do get more of a kick out of people singing along to 'News At Ten' or 'Letter From Hiro.' When I don't have to sing because the crowd are audible above the band and word perfect, I love that."

The band continued to gig regularly, and in May of that year returned to The Marquee to play two sell out shows on the 10th and 11th of May. Saturday 10th May was a memorable day for me. The football team I had supported since the age of 7, and who I had been as passionate about in my teenage years as I had been about my music (and who I would support more fervently in my adulthood once finances, the shackles of childhood and my temporary dwindling interest in live music permitted) had reached their third successive FA Cup Final. Fortunately, I was unable to watch their capitulation, as I was playing cricket, which had become a regular summer weekend activity by then. It also happened to be my mother's birthday, but with an ungratefully entitled matter of fact teenage sense of reasoning I figured that this wouldn't be any reason not to ask her to pick me up at the end of the cricket match and drop me at the station so that I could get up to London for the gig. She dutifully obliged, picking me up from the ground in Crawley where I'd been playing, packing a Fred Perry shirt, pair of jeans, Adidas trainers and a home-prepared sandwich into a bag on my behalf. I clambered into the car, changing out of my afternoon's white sporting uniform and contorting into my evening's mandatory gig outfit whilst demolishing the sandwich in the back seat of the car on its five-minute journey to Three Bridges station. Kev made his own way up from Haywards Heath, and we met at what was to become a very regular nominated rendezvous point, the Victoria Station branch of Our Price Records, perched on the edge of the main station's concourse just twenty yards from the steps down to the Victoria Line.

A short tube hop to Oxford Circus, the now familiar stroll east along Oxford Street and right turn down Wardour Street, and we were once again inside what had become as close to being a spiritual home as we had at that time. We grabbed a drink, headed to the front, took up a place stage right for no other reason than there was a bit of space there, and awaited the arrival of the support band.

Once again, we got talking to some of our fellow audience members, this time able to contribute our own Vapors memories to those related to us excitedly by likeminded individuals. We met Sarah, from Streatham, with a slightly spiky-haired, faintly punk-like appearance, who spoke with a strong, somewhat drawling South London accent, that coupled with her looks, tinted spectacles and fashion-sense immediately reminded us of media-darling of the time Janet Street-Porter. "Some people say I remind them of Janet Street-Porter," she informed us, instantly removing the opportunity for either of us to trot out what I imagine would have struck Kev and myself as a hilarious observation but in reality would presumably have been just a clumsy teenage rehash of a cliché she'd heard a thousand times over and was probably pre-empting. We discussed our hometown situations, our overall point-of-life circumstances, and of course our musical loves. Unsurprisingly Sarah's tastes were not dissimilar to ours, and we compared notes on our individual initial familiarisation landmarks up to that early point in the Vapors journey. We were joined in our conversation by Julie, another nascent Vapors fan from Beaconsfield, in Buckinghamshire, who like us had been introduced to the band through an already burning passion for The Jam.

The support band came and went, the between-set DJ spun the usual chosen-for-the-occasion, mood-matching mix of relevant, contemporary and exhilarating records that were almost as much a part of regular Marquee nights as the bands themselves, and we continued chatting with our new friends. Two guys from Bounds Green in North London joined in with the four of us as we chatted about anything and everything. One was Rudi, a tall, paisley-shirted, well-groomed, unmistakably fully-fledged mod, who shared my footballing allegiances and was also using the gig to overcome the afternoon's disappointment. The other was Colin, who shared Kev's dubious footballing loyalty, and the two of them combined to pepper Rudi and myself with the spirited sympathy that only Spurs fans can truly muster when Arsenal have slipped up, as they had done that afternoon against West Ham. Footballing differences dealt with, they too joined the music conversation and another couple of kindred spirits were very quickly identified.

The Vapors played, we got ever more involved, once again carried along by a fully on-board and fanatical audience, but now with growing familiarity of the songs and the band delivering them. The set finished, and we compared notes on our planned journeys home, all of us needing to head back to the tube before we disappeared to our respective locations in outer London and the home counties. Sarah advised us not to leave yet. "If we hang around in the bar, the band normally come out to say hello", she informed us in a matter of fact way. I'd never have described myself as being particularly starstruck or over-impressed by fame, although I have no idea how I would have reacted if I'd met Noddy Holder or Gary Glitter a few years earlier. Any awestruck reaction to meeting famous people had been knocked out of me, traumatically, when my dad had taken me to work with him one day at BBC TV Centre and Keith Chegwin blew a completely non-amusing fart-sounding party blower in my face for no good reason that I can remember, and then laughed hysterically. Weird. However, the opportunity to meet the members of our deliberately-adopted new favourite band was too good an opportunity to miss, and Kev, Colin, Rudi, Julie and myself dutifully followed Sarah to the bar, where we hung around awkwardly with no money to actually pass over it, waiting to meet them. Any casual relaxation and sense of belonging that we had felt inside the auditorium quickly evaporated into nervous feet-shuffling and desperate failures to strike cool, unconcerned poses as we stood and waited. The demographic of our immediate surroundings switched from similar-aged, awe-struck fans to older, alcohol-swilling seen-it-and-done-it apparent rock and roll veterans (the sort of whom we would of course, metamorphosise into in a handful of years' time, but at that age there was still a lot of growing up to do).

After a while, the band emerged from the venue's matchbox-sized dressing room through the door that led directly to the side of the bar, and did exactly what Sarah had promised, they made a point of saying hello. We spoke at length with Steve and Ed, who were as interested in why we were there and what we were all about as we were in their band stories, fundamentally of course because they were just bloody nice blokes (and remain so today). Nevertheless, it stands out as an exciting moment, meeting real life pop stars at length for the first time in any way other than a staged environment or as a passing hello, and finding them to be likeable, down to earth guys not so different from ourselves, who just happened to be pretty cool because they were in a band.

As we were about to leave, Steve asked if we were coming to the following night's show, a question to which we reluctantly had to respond negatively, explaining that our fifth form finances wouldn't stretch to another gig until the following week's paper rounds and odd jobs had restocked them. In the same breath, without breaking rhythm, Steve continued "Well if you can get here, we can always get you in on the guest list."

We attempted as best we could to maintain our nonchalant, ever so slightly pretty vacant demeanours, but it was impossible to react in any way other than with excited, youthful, appreciative, marginally disbelieving stacks of gratitude for the first of many favours and acts of kindness afforded us by the band over the forthcoming twelve months.

Kev and I spent the train journey home planning in fine detail the optimal level of money-scrounging and fare-dodging that we felt could balance practicality and necessity, and whatever plans, lost in time, that we hatched, bore fruition as we arrived same time, same place, the following evening. Compared to our first entrance to the venue five months earlier, we were ten-foot-tall swaggering pillars of confidence as we stooped at the glass window of the entrance kiosk and stated nonchalantly "We're on the guest list, it's Sarah plus four," adding somewhat redundantly "We're two of the plus four" whilst our hearts beat nineteen to the dozen and we desperately hoped that Steve had remembered his offer. The tickets popped out accompanied by the now familiar metallic clunk of their dispensing mechanism, and we swanned, relieved, into the Marquee once more.

Our increasing familiarity with the songs accelerated, fresh from hearing them all the night before, and our burgeoning friendships began to grow. We chatted again to the band after the gig, and once again all made our way back home feeling that unique sense of contentment that comes from the knowledge that you've spent the evening with a bunch of new mates that you sense with a degree of certainty will become long-term, firm friends.

Colin, Sarah and Julie were to become regular gig buddies. Rudi less so, but like Sally from school, he too would return into my life several years later in a completely unanticipated manner. Steve, Ed, Dave and Howard were also to feature hugely in the next year of my life, and three of the four also to return many, many years later.

The Marquee remained a special, special place for many years to come. There were further Vapors gigs there, regular repeated visits to see other bands that played there on multiple occasions who formed a part of my "regulars" list, and equally as many one-off performances from bands that formed a central part of those times and whose records I had bought in number. There were bands I knew less about but had thought may be interesting through reading articles about them and bands who I knew absolutely nothing about but went to see anyway because I had a spare evening and where better to spend it than at The Marquee Club. The formula always stayed the same, support band followed by 30 minutes of house-DJ selected crowd-appropriate tunes, headline act, and out by 11.00. The pitch-black, sweaty, sticky interior never changed. The bar layout, the smell of burgers drifting from the small kitchen at the back and the cramped loos were all a constant setting for several years of good-time gig going, and even now it's likely that I attended more gigs at that place in those few years than I have ever mustered at any other venue over the passing of the years since.

Even with the emotionally gut-wrenching move from Wardour Street to its new location in Charing Cross Road in 1988 the venue maintained a great deal of its reputation and unique style, with the slightly larger and more comfortable accommodation being decked out in similar fashion and colours and the formula being strictly adhered to. After its demise in 1996 there were a handful of various resurrection attempts early this century, but the place is now as much a part of rock and roll history that will never return as so many other great names are on both sides of the Atlantic. But no-one who was there, and that is a lot of people, will ever forget it, and none ever speak of it without fondness and the cracking of a wistful smile.

Days In The Sun

In late March 1980, a few weeks before those May Marquee gigs, "Turning Japanese" had been at number 3 in the UK charts. That same week The Jam had been at number 1, with "Going Underground" retaining its top spot after spectacularly storming straight to that position on its release the previous week. A glance down the rest of that week's top 40 makes for a roll call of memories. It also represents a pretty illustrative subsection of my record collection and I am sure of many others from what was undoubtedly a very special time for those of us of a certain age and musical persuasion. Martha and The Muffins, The Lambrettas, The Beat, The Police, Squeeze, Blondie and UB40 were all in that same week's top 20. Within the top 30 were Siouxsie and the Banshees, Stiff Little Fingers, The Bodysnatchers and Secret Affair. Bad Manners and The Stranglers had songs in the top 40, as did Dexy's Midnight Runners, with "Geno" anchoring the chart at number 40 at the beginning of its eventual ascent to the pinnacle.

Even as it unrolled, it felt very clearly that an "our time has come" golden era was underway, at least in terms of music, and the inspection of history does nothing to dispel that sense. In June, "Start" would become The Jam's second successive number 1 single, and the record release that some of us had really been waiting for, the first Vapors album "New Clear Days" would finally be upon us. Produced by recording legend Vic Coppersmith-Heaven, whose name was so familiar to us from its appearance all over seminal records in our collection, most notably of course by The Jam, the album was complete and ready to go, and a July release date was set.

Before the album became available, a tour was arranged to promote it, culminating in a show at what would be the largest UK venue the band had ever headlined (and that, at least thus far, remains so), the almost as legendary as the Marquee, Rainbow Theatre in Finsbury Park. The band had played there before, on The Jam tour, but there was no doubting that for them to be topping the bill in that place was a special occasion for band and fans alike.

Dependent on who you talk to, and probably equally dependent on your glass half empty/glass half full demeanour, The Chords were added to the bill for this one night of the tour only, either to contribute to the end of tour big concert hall triumphant atmosphere, or to boost poor ticket sales.

No complaints from us on that front. I was already a big fan, and to this day would always consider "Maybe Tomorrow" as one of the best singles of that whole age, and "So Far Away" as a classic album, right up there in my all-time favourites list and which still gets regular listens today. The band were slightly ahead of the curve in terms of timescales when set against The Vapors, but their career ran a similar course. "Maybe Tomorrow" was the second single, but the one that put them firmly in the public eye, hitting the charts and making "Top Of the Pops" after building up a large and loyal live following, just weeks before "Turning Japanese" did the same for The Vapors. "So Far Away" was released a couple of months before "New Clear Days" and although for them a second album never arrived, they reappeared in various guises and forms over the years and are currently performing with original guitarist and songwriter Chris Pope having assembled a new band and performing the singing duties himself.

Their addition to the bill for the Rainbow show was a bonus. Their name was already entwined with that of The Vapors and there was endorsement from The Jam, Paul Weller having sung the band's praises. The Vapors had supported The Chords at their own Marquee show the previous year, and both acts had received loud and favourable press coverage and recorded well received Peel sessions, a barometer of musical fashion like no other of the time. Chris and Buddy Ascott, the band's charismatic drummer, became, and remain, friends with Steve and Ed. I owned all the records but had never got around to seeing them, so The Rainbow show became a very eagerly awaited next Vapors gig.

Truth be told, it's not a gig I recall an awful lot about. Although it was the first time I'd seen The Chords, I remember a lot more from subsequent gigs, and The Vapors' set too isn't one I recall as a classic compared against some of the others. I do recall sitting in a line in a row of seats halfway back in the stalls, and I do recall Sarah's antipathy towards The Chords, a band she vehemently insisted she couldn't stand, although this opinion was later to be reversed. Maybe it was the fact that the venue was seated, maybe it was the significantly less than full house not being able to generate anything more than a somewhat subdued atmosphere, or maybe it was just that it wasn't the normal small, sweaty, boozy location that by now comprised our regular gig habitat, but it wasn't a stand out night. It's certainly not the case that venues like The Rainbow can't generate an atmosphere; I saw both The Jam and The Who in that same auditorium on more than one occasion, and the crowd electricity in there was as good as it was anywhere else, but on the night of The Vapors gig it just didn't happen.

Although I do remember it not being a classic, I don't remember any real sense of disappointment or anti-climax. They can't all be perfect, and less than perfect doesn't make them poor. It was another gig ticked off, another night with friends, and another journey home fraught with nothing but anticipation as we now only had days to wait before the biggest record release of our young music fans' lives.

"New Clear Days" hit the shops and I don't think there had ever been another album before, and there certainly wouldn't be another, that was fetched home from Mastersound so rapidly, so carefully and with such expectation. Kev and I purchased our copies simultaneously, made our way back to mine to inspect them, and opened our respective copies up with the excitement of children attacking Christmas stockings at 5.00am in the morning, tempered with the care and sense of reverence afforded to the handling of sacred religious artefacts by aging holy men. Song order, lyrics, album credits, artwork, label detail, size of the grooves and pretty much anything else that could be visually observed were scrutinised before we even began to actually listen to the thing. And then we did so, absorbing polished, recorded versions of the songs we were now fairly familiar with from repeated live airings and radio sessions, and filling in the vocal gaps and misheard lyrics that had made their way into our hearts and minds along the way. And then we listened to it again. And again. And again. And again.

I'd spent far more time over the previous couple of years than I would ever have wanted to painstakingly, pointlessly and incomprehensibly learning speeches from Shakespeare for no apparent reason other than to recite them back at a staring, lifeless, humourless, robotic English teacher who assured me that doing so would enrich me, and probably more importantly, keep his "O" level English Literature pass quota at a respectable level. To this day I have no understanding or interest in pretty much anything that the bloody bard has to offer, but I can, however, still recite, word for word, precisely-pronounced syllable by syllable, and set to the exact rhythmic framework of their musical surround, every moment of the first published long-playing collection of eleven of David Fenton's songs.

The tunes we already knew and loved, the lyrical content we had partly picked up live, the context of some of the songs was understood, but in a time-honoured style, here was a guy who was singing about things I understood and connected with. The political overtones and analogies wrapped around some of the songs were relevant and fitted the mood of the time and the attitude of the masses, but closer to our reality was the fact that we were relatively regular young men growing up in a certain place in a certain time, and here were a bunch of songs documenting and articulating perfectly our world. Dave often provides deliberately calculated and non-precise answers when asked what certain songs are really about, most notably of course, as already noted, the song for which he is most well-known, his stock answer often being "It's about whatever you want it to be about" and that, really, is the point. These songs worked for us.

Nobody who ever lived in England and had ever set foot outside of their own house in the second half of the twentieth century can fail to have vivid memories of the slam-door train. These much-maligned stalwarts formed a central part of my teenage life and early adult years, and despite their perpetual tattiness, permanent musty smell and dust-magnet cloth seating, they exuded a majesty of their own as they clunked, clattered and rattled their way between Haywards Heath and Brighton and London and occasionally elsewhere. My regular travels started too late for my journeys to be steam-propelled, but only the most cold-hearted non-nostalgic modern traveller could dispute the spirit and grandeur that memories of the "Electric Multiple Unit" beasts evoke, which will never be recreated by the sleek but drearily practical suburban rail fleets of today.

These were essential vehicles for the young gig-goer, and facilitated a lot more besides, including of course the ability to actually get to see, as well as actually speak to, young girlfriends who may not have lived locally and, in some cases, who didn't have a telephone at home.

The song "Trains" is one of the highlights of the "New Clear Days" album, was always a live favourite, and continues to be so to this day. More often than not introduced crisply by various band members during concerts as being about "hanging around at railway stations" as it had been the first time we became aware of it, Dave has taken to giving the song a more considered, explanatory introduction these days, half-embarrassedly explaining that any references it may contain to "sweet sixteen" girlfriends were written forty years ago. He will then go on to explain for the benefit of younger members of the audience how hanging about at railway stations was indeed a central part in the lives of many of us, due to the lack of punctuality exhibited in equal measures by the aforementioned girlfriends, and the trains themselves, or more likely both of them, and point out that mobile phones didn't exist, so all you could really do was pace up and down and wait.

Dave's obsession with and mistrust of trains seems to have stubbornly persisted with him through life, perhaps due in part to having to endure the daily commuter grind into London for a long period of his legal career whilst living north of the capital in Harpenden.

Even in 2018 it still manifested itself in the unlikeliest of ways. Shortly after Branka and Dave had moved down to Worthing, we met for a quiet, relaxed lunchtime drink at a beach bar on Brighton seafront. It was a warm, sunny August Friday afternoon, with Brighton's regular weekend buzz and population intake slowly building and we drank cold beer outside in what could only be described as a chilled atmosphere overlooking the sea. At around 4.00 Dave announced, slightly perturbed, that if they left to return to Worthing at that point, they'd have to spend a few extra quid on top of their already paid for off-peak return rail tickets. Despite having it pointed out to him that this wasn't really a major issue in the grand scheme of things, he decided that it was too great a blocker to leaving before 7.00, and we promptly drank on for another three hours. How we actually got back to our respective homes remains unremembered, but at least the cost of Dave's extra five pints of Stella were offset by the cost of, and mental anguish caused by, the extra two or three quid an enhanced rail ticket would have set him back. Dave's clearly deeply-held resentment of the railway company's ticketing policy was at least matched by the frustration he displayed about a year later when Branka and I reminded him teasingly about the afternoon, only to have it revealed to him that in fact the peak travel time rule didn't hold true on Southern services along the coast, and it wouldn't have cost him any extra to travel home whilst still relatively sober.

It could be argued, of course, that Dave's rigid adherence to the regulations and by-laws of public bodies is admirable, although anyone who has ever made the short walk from Brighton station to the seafront in his company would probably argue otherwise as he diligently and doggedly stops at every road crossing to wait for the green man.

Back in 1980, however, he was not a moral guardian role model for me, just a bloke whose every song lyric I scoured for meaning and enlightenment. As was the case with every song on the album, we spent hours and hours back then scouring through the lyrics to "Trains" trying to understand what hidden meanings might exist in the references to exotic sounding events like "glycerine parties" contained within. Even later in life, my wife asked me what the song was about, suspecting it may contain a number of deep and dark drug references. It's reassuring to know that it's about, well, hanging about at railway stations. Never let it be said that the songwriters of the day weren't close to the suffering of their fans.

Every song on the album was dissected, considered, reassembled, re-interpreted and given our own context in the way that the English teacher could only ever have dreamed that we may do with some of the eternally dull prescribed "O" level "classics" we were forced to endure. And as soon as the school holidays allowed, we were up to London, to discuss with Colin, Sarah and Julie, the songs in further depth and detail. Sarah's particular favourite was "Spring Collection" and its bitchy references towards the trying-too-hard fashion efforts of its subject, one of many just out-of-reach girls that appeared in Dave's songs. The line "In your parachute suit that you bought in Portobello" was adapted by the five of us and yelled at the top of our voices at every subsequent Vapors gig to reflect the fact that Sarah had indeed bought, and could often be seen in, her very own parachute suit that she bought in Streatham High Road, which scanned perfectly as substitute lyrics.

"Turning Japanese" was on the album of course, as were second and third singles "News At Ten" and "Waiting For The Weekend" along with what is for me, and many others, the album's high-spot, closing track "Letter From Hiro."

"News At Ten", in my mind a far superior song, was released as the follow up to "Turning Japanese" and received substantial airplay before charting just outside the top 40. A "Top Of The Pops" appearance that would surely have guaranteed a high chart position the following week was booked, but in what the band often refer to being what was perhaps a turning point in the trajectory of their career together, promptly pulled when a strike at the BBC forced the cancellation of that week's show. Later in the year "Waiting For The Weekend" failed, in cricketing parlance, to trouble the scorers.

They headed off for an Australian tour and two separate American ones in the second half of 1980, where their trajectory was still on an upward incline, and where they were playing live shows to significantly sized audiences.

The five of us spent the summer getting to know one another better away from the context of the inside of venues, sharing our musical loves and experiences with one another, comparing notes on written articles and opinions and just generally socialising with each other and each other's friends. We discussed family, parents, schoolfriends, interests outside of music, and although neither Kev nor I had lived particularly sheltered lives, we had lived them in a suburban Sussex bubble and meeting people from different walks of life who lived elsewhere in the country, albeit not exactly distant, was rewarding and nurturing. Sarah lived in a South London maisonette backing on to the railway lines with her father. Colin lived with his parents in a Victorian North London terrace (in an area I was to move into and grow to love in the 90s), and Julie lived with her parents in a large detached house of some style in leafy Buckinghamshire. Julie staunchly refused to let on how her father had made his money, but Colin eventually found out, announcing to the partial astonishment but overriding amusement of Kev and I that he was a member of British Eurovision heroes Brotherhood Of Man. Julie was furious at our discovery, worried it would offend our punk sensibilities whilst failing to recognise that our backgrounds weren't dissimilar, whereas the rest of us thought it was actually quite cool. What Colin has never been able to satisfactorily explain is the motive behind the event that led to his discovery, namely that "I just happened to be looking at a Brotherhood Of Man record cover in Virgin one day."

Between the two American tours, the band slotted in a couple of homecoming Marquee gigs on the 31st October and 1st November, which offered a return to the pre-Rainbow triumphalism of previous gigs, and that resulted in closed doors way before showtime (there was no such thing as advance ticket purchase at the Marquee).

We caught up with Ed and Steve, who once again treated us like old friends after the shows, and arranged to meet them the following week at the Brighton Centre, where The Jam were playing two nights this time round, midway through their "Sound Affects" tour. Never let it be said that we were swayed by the behaviour of our peers, or more appropriately in this case by our heroes, but unwittingly the pair of them changed a significant part of our gig habits at the first of those Jam nights. We met, as arranged, in the bar, and had a few drinks, more of which I suspect were paid for by Ed and Steve than by Kev or I, adding to the guestlist debts and beer debts that I'm still conscious are probably not yet fully repaid, and sat chatting until what seemed like being perilously close to being time for The Jam to arrive on stage. Having not entered the auditorium early on, and Jam crowds being of the nature that they were, we were conscious that our chances of getting anywhere close to the stage were fairly remote.

"How far forward do you think we'll be able to get?" I asked everyone. Steve looked at me like I was mad, replying calmly "Well we'll be standing at the back, next to the mixing desk. The sound quality will be best there, especially in this place." He had a point, and coming from a professional musician and future career sound engineer it was a logic we couldn't dispute, especially as it came from a guy who definitely felt like a mate, but in whose company we still thought it was a pretty cool thing to be.

We spent the best part of the next two years bemusing any friends and acquaintances who accompanied us to gigs of any shape, sound or size (Vapors performances excepted of course) by heading straight to the mixing desk at show time with a swaggering, knowing and I would imagine enormously irritating shrugging dismissal of any protests they may have made, stating matter of factly that "Everyone knows you get the best sound there, so that's where we're going."

During the pre-gig drinking session, Kev had mentioned, purely conversationally, that he had really liked the promotional T-shirts that had accompanied the "News At Ten" single and regretted not buying one at the time whilst they were still available. The following week, whilst we were killing time in some way or another round Kev's house one evening, his father, a large, sometimes jovial but sometimes downright scary man, with a smouldering pipe permanently protruding from his mouth, emerged from the sacrosanct space of his study to tell Kev that there was "Some guy or another called Edward on the phone for you." Ed had recalled maybe having an odd "News At Ten" T-shirt knocking about at home, located it, and was calling to check Kev's address so that he could send it over. It was a small gesture, but it was a kind, special and meaningful one that neither Kev nor I ever forgot.

The next significant Vapors related phone call came the following February, when we were called to let us know that, having returned from the US where they had completed their tour and promptly mixed their second album, they were booked for a BBC Radio 1 "In Concert" recording as a precursor to the album release and associated tour. We were invited to the event, to be recorded at the BBC's Paris Theatre in Lower Regent Street. Whilst very different to legendary music venues, this place had a history of its own, and was spoken of in revered tones by my father whose work in BBC Radio had crossed paths with the location on many occasions. Classic radio comedy had been recorded within the theatre-cum-studio over the years, as had numerous made-for-radio concerts. Queen, Pink Floyd, Led Zeppelin, David Bowie and many more had performances recorded there, so the band were in exalted company.

The new album "Magnets" had been recorded in November of 1980, rapidly and under some pressure from the record company between US tours. It was then mixed by the band, with producer David Tickle, in studios in California the following January before their return home. Steve sums up the crazy journey he'd taken in the year since he was supporting The Jam on the way up the curve, recounting his overriding memory of the Los Angeles studios they were holed up in whilst mixing the record. "We were in studio 2. In studio 1 was bloody Barry White! The man! I said to the studio manager, 'I'd really like to meet Barry White!' And one afternoon he grabbed me, handed me a tray he was carrying, and said 'There you go, take Barry his tea.'" Barry would apparently take tea regularly at 4.00pm, and as Steve entered, he turned to him and asked, "Who are you?" "I just said, 'Oh I'm from England, we're mixing an album.' And he just replied 'Cool, can I have some tea?' and

I thought to myself, whatever happens from here on I'll always be able to say, 'I had afternoon tea with Barry White.'" Can't argue with that.

Away from the music, over those winter months, Kev and I had spent a lot of weekend time in London with Colin, Sarah and Julie, or they'd spent time in Sussex with us. Somewhere along the line, Julie and myself embarked on a very brief epic teenage relationship, which I vaguely remember starting somewhere along Oxford Street on a cold Saturday December morning whilst both out-on-our-feet exhausted after staying up all night at Sarah's following a secret Jam gig at the Music Machine in Camden which we had somehow managed to get tickets for. And somewhere else along the line I remember it fizzling out in a bleak shopping centre in High Wycombe, for reasons that escape me.

We remained a group very much of five for a while, however, and as this was still the era of punk, of doing it yourself, of getting involved and all that it entailed, we clearly had to form a band. Colin and I both had guitars, I had musical training courtesy of my mother and other teachers' miraculous stewardship of my chronic lack of keyboard proficiency through a Grade 5 piano exam, and Kev had a bass guitar but wanted to be a drummer. Julie, after all, came from a musical family, and Sarah, like all of us, was a fanatical music fan who brought an artistic, creative angle to everything, and was clearly therefore in a position to lead the singing. Quick as a flash, The Frantic Aardvarks were formed, and notepads were summoned as we began to look deep (very, very deep, and to no avail) into our creative hearts to see what would stir.

The only completed song I can remember was a punk classic called "Shops" which consisted of three chords and a list of retail outlets gleaned from a walk around town yelled quite loudly. The marketing machine kicked into life and the girls had a set of badges manufactured ready for our promotional assault. The world was saved from our musical onslaught after too many arguments between ourselves and the girls and of course the inevitable musical differences (there was far too great a difference between music and what we were doing).

I later learnt that the girls carried on, supplemented with Suzanne and Melissa, two Vapors fans who became a part of the larger group towards the end of the band's life, and did actually get as far as rehearsing. Their biggest claim to fame came when using Julie's father's home studio one day whilst his band were supposed to be working in there, reducing the Brotherhood of Man to having to hold band practice in the front room.

Kev, Colin and I also pressed ahead, actually getting so far as to learn a few chords. Colin stuck with guitar, I cranked up Kev's bass, and Kev himself borrowed some drums. We talked the school caretaker into letting us set up in one of the more remote prefabricated huts and serenaded the poor residents of the neighbouring housing estate with painfully out of time versions of any current songs that were simple enough for us to fathom. "'A' Bomb In Wardour Street," "She's Lost Control" and an alternative version of "Teenage Kicks" featuring my 12-year-old youngest sister on vocals are the only ones I recall. Our none-too-promising song writing expertise also produced some long lost near classics such as "Change to Nought", a song inspired in equal measures by Blondie's "11:59" and the digital display on Kev's dad's state of the art Betamax video machine at midnight as it, well, changed to nought. Apparently, it was a metaphor for the sudden trough in Kev's emotional state after some heart-breaking split with a girlfriend, as was "Comedown", our only attempt, and only failure, at producing a slow song.

And that was it for the Frantic Aardvarks, save for the somewhat astounding appearance in the 2016 sharing on Facebook of pictures posted by Rob Payne. Rob was a Vapors fan back then too, with whom the evidence suggests we must have been acquainted, who has followed them with the same vigour and intensity as I have since they reformed. And miraculously, there amongst the images of the Vapors badges and other timeless memories put online by him, was a picture of what is more than likely the last remaining Frantic Aardvarks badge. It had taken us 36 years but finally, there we were, stamped in history.

Spring Collection

All set for a new year of Vapors experiences, The Frantic Aardvarks reconvened in the Shaftesbury Avenue branch of McDonald's at lunchtime on the 25th February 1981 in advance of the "In Concert" recording. Our usual, far earlier than required arrival time, coupled with straight batting BBC security guards who very clearly weren't going to let us in until "The designated studio time as clearly stated here", meant we had several hours to kill with a scrap of pennies between us. We strolled up Wardour Street to pay homage to the Marquee club, carried on up to Oxford Street to wander around HMV and the Virgin Megastore, back down through Soho and kicked our heels around the early 80s pre-clean-up China Town streets, and back to McDonald's where our combined pennies stretched to two portions of that timeless, mouth-charring classic the McDonald's Apple Pie. Sharing these out between us, and probably because of the undoubted simultaneous immediate burning of five hungry teenage mouths, it remains one of the over-riding memories of the day.

The designated studio time as clearly stated duly arrived, and we took our beige-felted seats somewhere in the middle of the auditorium. The theatre was like no other, with the usual attention to lighting, both ambient and stage-adorning, redundant in an arena that was used only for radio. Instead, the ceiling's fluorescent tubed ceiling and bright interior space was criss-crossed with a patchwork of seemingly random cables, associated microphones and acoustics enhancing mechanisms of all conceivable shapes and sizes. The audience too was somewhat different to the usual Vapors crowd, comprising of a few regular fans, some familiar members of the Guildford contingent, and a large number of incongruously dressed suits and more casually attired constituents who we assumed were BBC personnel who were able to apply to attend such recordings.

The "In Concert" series was a regular weekly Radio 1 series whose content by 1980 and 1981 was dominated by English post punk and new wave acts that had hit the radio mainstream. The format was simple. There would either be one act, playing a full hour-long set, or there would be a headline act and a support act, with both bands' sets being compressed into the show's one-hour window. To our disappointment, this recording was to take the latter of the two formats, with a band called Private Lives comprising the opening act, meaning only a very short Vapors set would follow.

The concert was compered by a young Gary Crowley, who adopted a somewhat confusing style throughout the afternoon, switching youth TV wild-eyed enthusiasm and banter with serious, considered musical appreciation, directed far more greatly, to our immense indignation, towards Private Lives rather than The Vapors. Offering "shout outs" or whatever the corresponding 80s radio term was, we sensed an opportunity for free radio self-promotion and asked him to mention the Frantic Aardvarks. To our even greater ire this had somehow been translated into "A big hello to The Frantics from Guildford!" by the time he made the announcement.

Private Lives played their set, which seemed to last forever, and about which I recollect very little, other than it being a fairly immemorable group of pop songs that was a kind of Kajagoogoo meets Johnny Hates Jazz amalgamation of post New Romantic rubbish, the kindest description of which would be that it was ahead of its time. Their main crime that day, of course, was not being The Vapors, but that was hardly their fault.

Finally, The Vapors got to play, but the time constraints meant that a very short, seven number set was all that was performed, or recorded. It was, however, the first opportunity to catch polished, live versions of some of the songs that would appear on the new album. Three old classics were played, along with four new songs, one of them ("Jimmie Jones") being vaguely familiar having been prototyped previously, and others offering first new glimpses of the slightly differing nature of the new material. Ed strapped on a 12-string acoustic guitar for the album's title track "Magnets" and another previously unheard track "Daylight Titans" was included. The quartet was completed by "Spiders" which had just been released as the band's new single, but like its predecessor "Waiting For The Weekend" failed to make the UK charts. For the record, the B-side to "Spiders", "Galleries For Guns", remains my favourite Vapors song to this day.

The show was broadcast a couple of weeks later on 7th March 1981. Despite the fact that it had been a privilege to be invited to the event, to catch up with the band after their US adventures, and to see and hear the new songs performed, our sense of dissatisfaction over the whole event was neatly framed when the broadcast version spent as long focussing on Private Lives as it did on our boys. Gary Crowley sealed the deal with his closing comments which went something like "Thanks so much to the totally amazing Private Lives, and to The Vapors" and Colin, who through life has remained a calm, rational, tolerant and understanding human being, can still be instantly transformed into a snarling, aggressive ball of vitriol at the mere mention of Gary Crowley's name.

A couple of days before the Paris Theatre recording, the five of us had met up at a Jam gig at Crawley Leisure Centre, just up the road from Haywards Heath, this one squeezed in as one of a handful of UK shows scheduled before a European tour in the spring of 1981.

If our DIY musical efforts were a glorious failure, they pale into insignificance alongside our even more disastrous attempts at creating that other homespun staple of the time, the music fanzine.

We'd become keen readers and collectors of some of the latter-day punk and mod fanzines of the time, Tony Fletcher's legendary "Jamming!" magazine being a favourite given its close compatibility with all things Jam-related, and with Tony (and his bandmates in his own outfit Apocalypse) being South London acquaintances of Sarah. There were numerous other, less polished but equally as interesting DIY fan creations around, however, that helped spread the word about current non-mainstream musical trends and events. These frequently also included at times quite considered and well written fans' homages to historical records or concerts, gig reviews and interviews with musicians whose work we promptly researched further, usually in terms of seeking out the records they referenced. Colin's mod mate Rudi, who had been there back at those Vapors Marquee gigs, ran one such magazine with his equally out-and-out mod friend Chris, named Fightback, which of course we scoured religiously word for word.

We'd discussed amongst ourselves many times the need for us to get creative in this particular area without of course working out how we were going to do so or formulate any plans. The opportunity arose at the Crawley Jam gig to begin our journalistic adventure, which turned out to be even shorter than our career together as a band. For much of the rest of the spring, we would arrive during the afternoon of Vapors gigs in order to attempt to find a way into the venue during the soundcheck and shamelessly beg the band for places on the evening's guestlist. With The Jam, by this time, the practice of arriving early to gain entry to the soundcheck had become a regular feature for a much larger portion of their much larger audience. Not, in this case because any additional favours were being requested, the favour the band were doing to the fans by inviting a significant number in each afternoon to watch them set up and prepare was in itself a great gesture, but because it was one that merely enhanced the bond between group and followers which all contributed to each of their shows' great senses of occasion. It simply represented an opportunity to extend the feeling of being part of a very special alliance for those lucky enough to be ushered in via back doors, stage doors or loading ramps after milling about outside the venue since early afternoon.

With Crawley just on our doorstep, it was an easy decision to make to get there early, and Kev and I met up with Sarah, Julie and Colin and were dutifully ushered in via a side door and invited to come and watch the band run through their pre-gig set up routines. The sheer numbers attending these occasions meant that even these casual afternoon precursors to the main event carried a weight of expectation and had to be marshalled properly by venue staff and Jam road crew alike. In my memory this was always done with good grace, kinship and respect, not always qualities associated with some of the supporting personnel that keep the rock business infrastructure rolling in larger venues.

Our small assembled number took up various positions across the hall's floor as The Jam prepared, desperately trying to look as cool and unfazed as we could that we'd been invited in by the three guys on stage to whom we attached such devotion and for whom we had so much respect. I always recall not quite knowing how to behave in these circumstances, very aware that, unlike later on when the hall would be packed and lit for a rock concert, I was well within the eyeshot of the band, and therefore racked with teenage self-consciousness. Was it appropriate to dance to the half-performed, stop-start pieces of music they would run through as they got their levels, balances, monitors, amps and PA settings right? Should you applaud in the gaps between? Or should you wait until the end of the session when they'd play through two or three complete numbers, often ones that didn't always get aired in public or would not feature in that evening's show? In the end, I seem to remember adopting what I assumed, quite incorrectly I am sure, was a convincingly knowledgeable routine of looking concerned when various tweaks made by sound engineers or band members resulted in feedback or dropped bass or overloud guitar, or Weller would stop a song and ask for some change to be made to some frequency somewhere in some way or another. Maybe I subconsciously believed I was tapping into my father's sound engineering DNA as I then nodded knowingly and cast an eye around the speakers as if to acknowledge how someone's expertise in the intricacies of dial reading and knob twiddling was bringing the musical quality up to requirements. Truth be told, I probably behave the same way to this day when Steve is standing, bass strapped on and arms waving around at people, facing the stage and balancing noises at Vapors soundchecks.

Meanwhile, The Jam completed their preparations, and came to say hello to those of us lucky enough to have been inside the hall. I managed to get all three of them to autograph my "Sound Affects" T-shirt, something I was so proud of that I think I wore it, showing it off to the world as a whole, for the best part of the next two weeks, after which time I did the usual teenage boy thing of leaving it on the bedroom floor for later. My mum, being a mum, cleared it up with the rest of my detritus and gave it a good hot wash, removing any trace of the three hallowed signatures. Life lesson learnt.

Expecting to be ushered out of the venue until the doors opened to the public a couple of hours later, we were surprised to find that, as we had tickets for the evening, we were welcome to stay inside. Being a leisure centre, this afforded the ability to relax in the café, and play some pool. As we approached the pool table, we were delighted to see that it was occupied by the evening's support band, The Purple Hearts. By now they themselves were mainstays of the London mod scene and were a band we'd seen a couple of times the previous year and were fairly familiar with. Seizing the opportunity, Julie strayed over, surprising the rest of us more than the band members, by asking enthusiastically "Can we interview you for our fanzine?"

Caught somewhat on the hop by their eager, affirmative response, we found ourselves sat round a plastic table on plastic chairs with cups of plastic tea and blank looks aplenty.

"What's your fanzine called?" we were asked.

"Erm, not sure yet" one of us mumbled.

Further probing social intercourse followed.

"Have you travelled far to the gig?"

"Have you seen us before?"

"What other bands are you into?"

It struck me that this was probably not how fanzine interviews were usually constructed and that it would be more customary for us to actually be asking the questions of the band. The same thought obviously struck Sarah at the same time as she pulled a biro purposefully out of her bag, glanced around to see if anyone could muster a scrap of paper, and settled for a couple of folded paper napkins from the tea counter.

Poised and ready, she looked like she meant business as one of the band members requested, not unreasonably "Right, what do you want to ask us?"

Blank looks and silence followed, and all I remember having is a short, good natured chat at the end of which we were given the sound practical advice that "You might want to think about what it is you actually want to write about, and get one of those recording machines." We agreed that was a really helpful insight and thanked them for their time as they hotfooted it as fast as they could to the safety of their dressing room.

The output from the afternoon's research has yet to see the light of day.

In March 1981, The Vapors set out on what turned out to be their last UK tour, billed the "Mad March" tour and lined up to promote the "Magnets" album.

The album itself was clearly a progression from "New Clear Days". Whether it was any better or any worse is a matter of personal taste and opinion, certainly there are songs on there that have greater structure, are perhaps darker from a lyrical perspective, and which are more diverse in musical style, but the lack of immediacy that some of the tracks offered set against the contents of the debut record demanded a more staged absorption over time. I don't know if I have a favourite out of the two or not. I've never kept count of which has been played the most on my lifetime's succession of technologically evolving playback devices, but I do know they have both been very regular listening over the decades. At the time of its release, neither Kev nor I had the time to dissect and analyse it in such detail as we had its predecessor, due to being just too busy with college work, gigs, and earning the required spending money, however it was still studied and analysed with a reverence afforded to very few albums before or since.

By now we were a hardened bunch of rock and roll stalwarts. Sarah had reached the legal age for purchasing alcohol, Kev had turned seventeen, Colin and myself were nearing that advanced age of wisdom ourselves, and Julie was beginning to worry about impending "O" levels.

A pre-tour warm-up gig was booked at a Middlesex Polytechnic site in Hendon for a few days after that Jam gig in Crawley, and a month of intense Vapors gigging began. The Hendon gig set the tone for the tour. Turn up early, find a way in to the soundcheck, ask ever so politely for a freeloading guestlist place for the evening, enjoy the gig, chat with the band, go home. In fact, the locations of some of the gigs lent themselves quite well to the geographic locations of the five of us and we were able to stop at each other's houses as appropriate, which in reality, if the event was anywhere near London, meant all piling back to Sarah's at whatever hour it was, and sitting up chatting all night before feeling rubbish for the remainder of the following day. Each and every one of us, even those like my sister Suzi who would only have ever once or twice been a part of our earnest nocturnal discussions, recalls clearly to this day the rotating, metronomic pendulum motion of the carriage clock on Sarah's mantelpiece, which somehow conducted and directed our conversations.

We didn't all go to all of the gigs, some were at some, others were at others. I recall those at Guildford, Brighton, Birmingham and Watford amongst others, as well as the two London shows that closed the tour. Halfway through the tour we met Suzanne and Melissa, who joined us at every other subsequent gig, and became a gang of four with Sarah and Julie for the rest of the tour. Suzanne recalls with amusement how the four of them each had to nominate a favourite Vapor and "Typically, I was left with the drummer" which seems a little harsh given that Howard was as nice a guy as the rest of them. Their individual allegiances were then worn, literally, on their sleeves, for the rest of the tour as they turned up at each gig with handmade glove puppets of their own adopted band member which were held aloft at the front of each gig and joined in the fun, Punch and Judy style.

The Brighton gig, of course, was a special occasion for Kev and myself, not only because we managed to persuade some college mates along to see what the fuss was all about, but also because The Chords had once again been slotted in for a guest appearance, this time in order to give them a debut to new singer Kip, once of The Vibrators, ahead of going out to perform their own headline shows with their new line-up.

Amongst our number that evening was Pete, a friend of Kev's who has remained in touch ever since and has also attended a number of the reunion gigs since 2016. He used the opportunity to present Ed with a demo tape of his college band at the time, who I vaguely remember as being half decent. Pete enquired with a chuckle at The Vapors' 2017 100 Club gig 36 years later of Ed whether he had ever listened to it, which, to Ed's credit was met with a straight-faced, dryly delivered "Funnily enough I was just about to get to that one."

Support band for the tour was a group hailing from Newcastle called White Heat. Fronted by the self-styled "Geordie Springsteen", a physically incapable of standing still show-off named Bob Smeaton and his livewire song writing partner and guitarist Alan Fish, the band performed a high energy but full-bodied melodic set of rock tunes that instantly appealed. Ably accompanied by a boisterous, energetic, full sounding accomplished group of musicians including something as exotic as a saxophonist, they immediately impressed from the start of the tour, and contributed greatly to each and every gig.

Smeaton himself, we learned to no-one's real surprise, was a minor celebrity on Tyneside who, according to local legend at least had stormed the stage during a Bruce Springsteen concert and been invited to share vocals, although the suspicion was that The Boss may not have been given the choice. Videos can be found of White Heat performances on YouTube, which remind those of us who remember them fondly just how much energy went into the performances. Bob would spurn the opportunity that a twenty second instrumental break affords most singers to take a quick breather by instead squeezing in a quick twenty front of stage press-up routine whilst the rest of the band kicked, leapt and bounced. A single album and a handful of singles were unfortunately all the recorded material that emerged during the band's lifetime, but they were a hugely popular live act in the North-East, with a number of loyal Geordies often making the trip to their London gigs later on that year and the next. They played their own headline shows at The Marquee after The Vapors tour, and their shows became regular events for Kev, Colin and I long after The Vapors' demise.

Like Ed, Bob Smeaton eventually turned his talents to screen direction, focusing on the music world, and he has an impressive list of credits as well as Grammy awards and Emmy nominations. A heavyweight list of TV movies and documentaries bear his name encompassing Hendrix, The Beatles, and almost inevitably "About The Young Idea", the 2015 Jam retrospective, amongst others.

As the tour progressed, and despite the addition of others to the group of regulars we associated with at gigs, the cracks amongst our number were beginning to show. Sarah was growing weary of our teenage boys' general uselessness and dependence on her streetwise knowledge of London music venues and bus routes. She began to resent our ungrateful and never-ending assumption that it was OK for us to kip on her sofa after we had spectacularly failed to factor in practicalities such as suburban rail timetables to our gig planning.

Julie and myself were finding it even more difficult to communicate than we had done during our long-dead fledgling six week teenage romance, and gradually the five of us became three and two, split neatly along gender lines, with the two factions competing publicly at gigs to demonstrate to each other how cool we were by attempting to impress anyone that cared to pay any attention to us and adding them to our group of friends.

Things came to a head at Roehampton, the final gig of the "Mad March" tour, held in a hall at the Froebel Institute (now part of Roehampton University), a homely small-style campus college situated in the deepest suburbs of South-West London, set amongst landscaped parkland that happened, on that particular day, to be awash with yellow daffodils gleaming in the spring sunshine. I can't remember the reason for the argument, but long before either of the bands played, we'd split into two non-conversant blocs, Julie and Sarah doing their best to ignore the three of us whilst befriending anyone they could in the crowd, whilst Kev, Colin and myself tried, with a not-so-astonishing lack of success, to look cool and not care that the girls wouldn't talk to us.

We had arrived early, on a bus. I can't remember exactly where we got the bus from, but the route would undoubtedly have been planned painstakingly by Sarah and would probably have involved getting ourselves to Brixton tube station from which point on we would have fallen under the control of her tour operations. The bands had yet to soundcheck, and we walked into the auditorium with our usual combination of brash teenage arrogance and just-below-the-surface nervousness about getting challenged as to our legitimate reason for being there and getting thrown straight out again.

Fortunately, we spotted Steve and Ed straightaway and negotiated our places on the guest list for the evening, which was arranged with the now customary good grace and friendliness that our take-it-for-granted presumptuousness certainly didn't warrant. As it was the last night of the tour, Kev's mum had been cajoled into making a cake decorated spectacularly with the cover of the "Spiders" single that we hoped might in some way demonstrate at least some of the gratitude that we felt for all of the guest list entries and free beers that the band had provided over the past year, and we managed to get one of their crew to smuggle it into the dressing room for post-gig presentation.

The gig evening became increasingly memorable as it wore on. White Heat played their usual blistering support slot, during which, unbeknown to anyone else, various members of The Vapors' entourage terrorised their dressing room in a last night of the tour prank, mimicking one previously played upon themselves by The Jam, seizing all of their belongings and gaffer-taping them to the ceiling. Revenge would follow during The Vapors set, but not before the power had given out during one of its early numbers, "Jimmie Jones". Whilst the band looked bemused at each other as various student entertainment staff strutted nervously around trying to look like they had the situation under control, the unexpected silence gave time for more cringing teenage posturing between the now firmly splintered Frantic Aardvark factions. Dave remembers trying to take control, leading the crowd into a mass singalong of the song's chorus, but neither he, nor I, have any recollection of the success, or otherwise, of this impromptu participation attempt.

Power restored, The Vapors continued their set, to be joined late on by a retaliatory stage invasion from White Heat, all of them stripped completely naked with the exception of a handful of strategically placed daffodils ripped from the beauty of the earlier spring sunshine and doomed to a premature demise as they fell from the variously sized body parts they were supposed to be protecting to be crushed on the stage floor.

By the end of the gig, we'd spent our last few pennies on however much cheap beer we could muster between the three of us, and the tranquil sunny afternoon mood had given way to a boozed up cheery celebration after the chaos of the gig carried over to the end of tour party, and cake presentation, that followed.

At about half past midnight, it dawned on the three of us that the last bus had probably left, even if we had actually retained enough money to board it. The girls had long gone, although it was fairly obvious that any chance of staying round Sarah's that night had departed several hours previously anyway, and the band were packing up and leaving.

And so, the thorny issue of how to get home had to be confronted.

We had no choice other than to exit the campus grounds, emerging onto Roehampton Lane, and vaguely remembering which way the bus had come from. Consequently, it seemed logical to reverse that direction, and we set off northwards with no real idea of where we were, or indeed where we were headed. We saw a road sign indicating that we were probably staggering towards Hammersmith, and my nascent geographical knowledge of the city (learned entirely from the Underground Map and the location of gig venues) kicked in. Hammersmith was on the same tube line as Victoria, and furthermore we'd seen bands there. It seemed entirely plausible therefore that if we managed to get there, we would be able to follow some unmarked straight line to Victoria Station from where we could bunk a train home in the morning.

I'm not sure what our logic was, perhaps we intended to hug the ground listening to echoes from the tunnels to keep us level with the tube line below, but it was never tested as we soon reached the South Circular Road and changed our plan. We knew that this thoroughfare also traversed the top of Brixton Hill, as we'd crossed it several times on the bus trips to Sarah's, and furthermore, Brixton was also known to us as a gig location, and a directly accessible tube journey from Victoria, but with fewer stops, so reason followed that this would be an even easier route to navigate.

Events overtook us once more, however, as we left the leafy darkness of the Roehampton section of the road and arrived at the bleak, concrete end of Putney. Another road sign helped us, directing us left towards Chelsea, a place that we knew was definitely near Victoria, because some kids from school went there to watch football, and they had told us how easy it was to get to. No matter that the Chelsea ground is actually in Fulham, the sign did its job, and we walked up Putney High Street, a place that these days would still be alive at that time of the morning, but was long since deserted somewhere between 2.00am and 3.00am in March of 1980. We crossed Putney Bridge, triumphant in our innate sense of worldliness, reasoning that we were now able to use ancient directional instincts to follow the river if necessary as we were also aware that it passed quite close to our now agreed target.

River navigation was unnecessary as we encountered a further road sign directing us up the New Kings Road, and we route-marched its entire length, into the actual Kings Road, through actual Chelsea, and up to Sloane Square, where, shining from above like an almost touchable holy grail, we glanced upon a road sign directing traffic to Victoria Station.

We reached Victoria at about 4.30am, and slumped on to a bench, shortly to realise that there was an imminent departure to the Sussex Coast that stopped at Haywards Heath. Kev and I jumped on board, leaving poor Colin to sit by himself in the overnight squalor of the deserted, save for a few rough sleepers and assorted undesirables, concourse, to wait for the Victoria Line to open a couple of hours later and ferry him home. To be fair, I don't feel too guilty, Colin still hails our out-of-town navigational genius, fully admitting that he would have had no idea of the route he should take. I was disappointed to work out recently that the walk can only have been about six miles long, however at the time it did feel just the tiniest bit heroic.

The Vapors played two UK gigs after the tour had finished, one at Lanchester Polytechnic in Coventry on 30th April, and a warm-up gig the previous week at The Royal in Guildford. The girls went to the Guildford gig however neither Kev, Colin nor I did, and we tuned in keenly the following week to listen to the live show broadcast on Richard Skinner's evening Radio 1 show. The band then headed off once again to the US where their popularity was still running high, and where the final single "Jimmie Jones" was beginning to achieve some success.

America was still a distant and remote place for South-East suburban teenagers, but one that was by now familiar through our absorption of rock music's evolutionary history, and equally what was happening over there musically at that point in time. Unavoidably, current affairs also began to inform our knowledge of all things USA, as the constant bombardment of world news and seemingly inevitable nuclear apocalypse continued apace.

But in the US too there were any number of teenage music fans, discovering their own tastes and identities within that country's culture in exactly the same way as we were doing.

Evan Blonder was one such young, stateside music lover.

Evan cites The Beatles as his first (and still greatest) musical love. "I was nine when they split, and I was beside myself!" he laments. Through the seventies he trod the well-worn path of radio-music absorption, getting into fairly mainstream rock acts such as Foreigner, Led Zeppelin and The Who, all the while learning their songs on the guitar. "And then when I was up in Buffalo at college, there was this guy across the hall listening to all crazy stuff and I'd just sit outside his dorm room and ask him 'What is all that?'" He recalls learning about any number of diverse future musical loves in this way; Joe Jackson, The Cars, The Pretenders, The Police, The B52s and Grace Jones are just some of the names that spring into his memory. "Then every day became a trip to the record store!"

As a 17-year-old college student Evan began dating a girl called Rebecca. "She lived on the Upper West Side of Manhattan and she was a Vapors fan" he recalls. "She had all these friends, we used to go downtown like in the Village, just go walking around, finding something to eat, that kind of thing. And then one time she looks to her right into a record store and sees the import of 'Turning Japanese' in the window. I knew nothing of it, but she just pulls me by the arm and runs into the store and asks me to buy her the single." He cracks into a slightly cheeky mid-fifties version of a boyish grin before adding "I'm 17 and I'm like dating this 19-year-old girl so of course I'm going 'Sure I'll buy it for you!'"

So they bought the record, took it home and listened to it. "I loved it, and we turned it over and played 'Talk Talk'" he continues (the song having been used instead of "Here Comes The Judge" as the B-side of the American version). "And I'm like, who are these guys? And she just says 'Oh, they're The Vapors from England.'"

He was hooked from that moment on. "I'm like, right, when are they coming over? I've got to see them! But we're waiting and waiting, and they never come." With that summer over, he moved to the University of Maryland near Washington DC to take up a place in veterinary school. Now separated from Rebecca, but whilst living in the DC area, The Vapors finally got to play in New York, but distance and student finances meant that Evan was unable to make the trip up north to see them. "I did at least meet another fellow at University who was into The Vapors, we both already had 'New Clear Days' and we went out together to buy our copies of 'Magnets' when it was released." But further near misses on American tour dates followed, and to his great regret, he never got to see the band he describes as "Band number 2 in my life, behind only The Beatles" before their demise.

His time was to come.

Back in New York City, in the late sixties, Bobby Weiss was born. Moving upstate to Westchester County when he was two, Bobby grew up in a musical family. His father, George David Weiss, was a noted songwriter with a staggering CV of credits to his name, numbering such timeless classics as "Lullaby of Birdland", "Can't Help Falling In Love" and "What a Wonderful World" amongst them.

Like so many of us, Bobby knew he loved music early on, and spent time honing and refining his tastes, before discovering, with a bang, the styles and genres that would shape his life.

"I went straight from Disney records to Kiss!" he laughs. "That was quite life-changing. I went from having those great big colourful Disney soundtracks and gazing at all the colours and pictures on the gatefold packaging as I listened to the songs from the films overnight one Christmas when I got a couple of Kiss records as presents."

Bobby was instantly into rock and roll, and in subsequent years would play guitar in any number of variously styled bands, all at the heavier end of the spectrum. "A lot of subsequent bandmates cite Kiss as the band that got them up and playing for themselves," he explains, "but for me, the moment I decided I needed to form a band was when I was just eleven, and I heard 'New Clear Days' for the first time." He hesitates, before continuing "Yeah, that was my life-changing moment actually. I put that record on and front to back I fell in love with The Vapors, every single song. I'd come home from school every day, stand in front of the microphone stand that my dad had given me with no microphone in it and sing along to the album, sometimes twice in a row. After that I just knew I had to put a band together."

Like many contemporaries both in the US and back here in the UK, Bobby had got into the band's music at a time when they were touring, but when he was just too young to actually go and see them play. And once old enough, they were no more.

Like Evan, however, his time was also to come.

The band completed their final US tour over the summer of 1981, before returning home.

It would be thirty-five years before any of us got to see The Vapors perform live again.

Cold War

Although technically not a live performance, our last encounter with the band came at The Tabernacle in Notting Hill Gate, to where we had been invited along with a group of other fans to help out as extras for the crowd scene in the promotional video for "Jimmie Jones".

Fortunately, this Julien Temple directed cinematic classic is still widely available on the Internet, and viewing it confirms the overriding memory of that evening, which is of a completely bonkers few hours listening to and watching countless takes of mimed sections of the song whilst various directorial touches were added to the stage performance and crowd behaviour alike. Dave, Ed and Steve all have almost identical responses when questioned as to their recollections of the evening, which run something like "All I remember is those bloody chickens." Anyone who was there, or is familiar with the video, will understand this sentiment, but the best way of otherwise describing the relevant content is to direct the reader to YouTube where they can enjoy 3 minutes and 26 minutes of rock and roll history for themselves. Suffice to say, watching Ed's balancing act whilst avoiding stray poultry during his customary leg kicks and exaggerated foot tapping is up there amongst the best in British slapstick comedy.

The red-brick, circular Tabernacle was founded in 1869 as a protestant place of worship, but during the 1970s had been given over as a multi-purpose council run neighbourhood space. These days, after a couple of subsequent refurbishments, it is a thriving local arts centre, supporting music, cinema, exhibitions, bars and a restaurant, and numerous community events. Its history from the 1980s onwards makes for impressive reading, being a large focal constituent of the Notting Hill arts and music scene and its strong ties to the carnival. The roster of musicians having used the space includes the likes of Joe Strummer and Damon Albarn in his "The Good, The Bad and the Queen" and "Monkey" opera guises, and it also professes to be one of the birthplaces of the British rap movement, no minor assertion.

In 1981, however, it still resembled a fairly typical Victorian place of worship, with a slightly creaky and ever so slightly unnervingly wobbly wooden interior combined with the musty smell of churches the length and breadth of the country. Bored of the chickens and the umpteenth instruction to sway in choreographed syncopation with our fellow fans to a 20 second segment of the song, Kev and I made our way up a rickety staircase at the back of the hall with Chris and Buddy from The Chords, who had come along for the evening's entertainment as well. At the top we found ourselves on a small balcony separated from the auditorium below by a perilously quivering handrail that looked, and felt, like it would give way if we so much breathed at it or a rogue rooster freed itself from Ed's boots and found its way up there.

We were delighted to find a couple of stowed away fold-out wheelchairs, of the fabric seated and pram-like wheeled variety that were used in public places back then, and the four of us spent the rest of the evening taking turns to push each other at ever-spiralling reckless speeds along the balcony, waving and gurning towards the cameras in the hope that we'd somehow be spotted during the final cut of the video at the back of one of the crowd shots. Sadly, despite painstaking studies of the released version I've yet to see any evidence of our wonderfully puerile twenty minutes of fun.

Schoolboy humour exhausted, we retired to the pub, heading into a traditional (in the least quixotic sense of the word) brightly lit, smoke filled concrete neighbourhood bar slapped like a seeming afterthought for the masses to relax in onto the edge of a hastily built post-war estate somewhere in the Notting Hill hinterland. We didn't quite get the full on, room silencing set of stares that could often accompany walking into the wrong pub back in those days, but our relative youth, mod-dressed attire and ordering of four pints of lager were accompanied by stony glares from all corners, including from behind the bar, by the exclusively male, surly inhabitants. Completely oblivious of the fact that we were wholly in the midst of first-generation Irish immigrants of a certain age, most likely primarily comprised of practising, or at least conformant, Catholics, we began cracking jokes aimed at Chris Pope about how lucky he'd been that day (in Rome, the actual Pope had survived an assassination attempt, but suffered some quite severe bullet wounds). As the scowls turned to growls, we were shaken out of idiot mode and left the pub quickly. Kev and I were both slightly disappointed to see our cool, streetwise, rock star drinking buddies decide that it was time to leave so soon, but it seemed best that we hot-footed it to the safety of the tube station.

"Jimmie Jones" was released, charted in the low 40s and spawned a "Top Of The Pops" appearance. By this time, I was somewhere deep in the German Alps on a camping holiday with some sixth form friends that didn't include Kev amongst their number. Desperate for news on chart update day, the following Tuesday afternoon I wandered the mile or so to the nearest payphone armed with Deutschmarks and checked in with him, excited to learn just how big a second hit single The Vapors were finally getting to have. My holiday mojo was pretty much ruined for a good couple of days or so afterwards as Kev broke the news that the record had slid into oblivion.

Later that summer, news broke that the band had called it a day. Dark rumours and theories spread amongst fans about who had heard what, and the circumstances surrounding the split, but the reality was, as is well documented, that it had just come to a natural end. The record company had pulled the plug on the studio time booked to produce a new single without informing the band. With United Artists having been taken over by EMI the previous year and the band having been shifted to the latter's Liberty Records subsidiary, all links with the personnel that had supported and promoted the band, both internally to the company and externally to the public, had long been removed. Despite the live popularity of the band, at least in the US, the lack of commercial success for the last single and the "Magnets" album contributed to their sense of having seen it through, and that was that. Ed describes his original spell as a Vapor in simple, happy terms. "We had two great years, for the first year we were the luckiest band in the world and for the second, one of the unluckiest" he reasons, neatly drawing the line under the band in a simple, bitterness-free statement of closure.

For Dave, it seems that the primary frustration was the demise of the vehicle that had allowed him to successfully demonstrate his first love, song writing, to the world rather than the loss of rock star status and the associated recording and touring treadmill. He still wears a look of disappointment as he describes how the reality began to set in about the way they had effectively been abandoned by their record company and the fact that nobody from EMI/Liberty had even afforded them the decency of being straight with them. "I really wanted to get a third album together" he recalls, but the promise of being able to continue to write and develop songs in whatever guise came next was compensatory in this respect.

Steve freely admits to having no idea what he was going to do himself, whilst Ed took the view that he'd had a blast, but as the youngest member of the band knew exactly where he was heading, which was back to college, film school to be precise, and train for what was to become his lifetime career.

Unlike the others, Howard made a conscious decision to withdraw from the frontline, his last gig as a musician being the last Vapors gig in San Francisco. He did, however, stay within the industry where he worked for the Performing Rights Society, the organisation that represents songwriters and publishers.

Popular wisdom has it that Dave immediately resorted to his pre-Vapors professional training and took up his law career, but in reality, this was still several years away, and he continued in the music business in various guises through the next decade.

In the meantime, Kev, Colin and myself needed urgently to apply ourselves to the task of finding a replacement band to adopt. At the time, I remember shrugging my shoulders a little when the band split, and it not being the bombshell that it would perhaps have been had it happened just a few months earlier. We were growing up fast, money was becoming easier to earn, and to spend, and we were now completely savvy with the London gig scene and familiar with an ever-expanding set of bands that were playing the exact sort of venues that constituted a perfect evening's location for our obsession. Certainly, looking back, the sense of disappointment at the loss of The Vapors pales into insignificance with the upset of Paul Weller's announcement of his dismantling of The Jam a year later, but the reality is that the latter event heralded the end of an era, rather than just a constituent part.

Onwards and upwards, and The Vapors had a ready-made replacement in our hearts in The Chords. As much as the music, the friendships made, the camaraderie, participatory feel and familiarity engendered by repeated, regular gigs had fuelled our Vapors obsession, there was another factor at play too. Our fragile teenage egos enjoyed the kudos that we believed existed amongst our peers brought about by the fact that we knew a bunch of real, live, actual rock stars. With their close association to The Vapors, their friendship with the band, and our also frequent trips to their shows, and of course the fact that we loved their music, The Chords quickly, and obviously, albeit briefly, took over the top of our league table.

Whilst The Vapors are, in some quarters, loosely, and in my opinion entirely inaccurately, associated with the whole mod revival of the time, largely due to their association with The Jam (and indeed The Chords), Chris and Buddy's band were firmly tied up with, and a big constituent part of, that whole movement. This suited us perfectly, having decided in a very calculated and deliberate way by then that this was the faction within the divided youth culture of the time within which we were going to slot ourselves. It's probably the only time in my life when I have really bothered about taking my attire in any way seriously, and although driven by the music and the events of the time, it became more than just a desperate need for a couple of teenagers searching for an identity to take out into the world. We delved very deeply into the scene that existed in both Brighton and London, and spent enormous amounts of time researching, and falling in love with, the music of the past that had generated it the first time around. For sure the tonic jackets, pressed white trousers and Jam shoes stayed at home for Vapors gigs when Harringtons and Fred Perrys were more than enough, but a lot of time was also spent in clothes shops looking at unaffordable accessories to supplement the few we had been able to muster.

The Chords played a couple of shows at The Marquee that autumn, which we attended adopting our Vapors-style approach of wandering round the back, strolling into the soundcheck and blagging a slot on the guest list. They had recorded a couple of new singles with Kip on board that flopped badly, played these two gigs and then promptly split up themselves. Perhaps subconsciously worrying that I was becoming some form of kiss of death, I don't think there has ever been a time since when I could definitely answer the question "Who's your favourite band then?" with a succinct one-word answer, but maybe I just grew up a bit more in my eighteenth year. There were certainly bands that became oft-repeated regulars on my gig lists, but the whole fandom thing began to be a little more relaxed and less obsessive from that point on, up until 2016 at least.

Months after our near self-inflicted brush with bother with the elderly Irish community in Notting Hill, it was after the last of those Chords gigs that I experienced one of my thankfully few encounters with violence. Slightly over-boozed and full of teenage bravado, I sat on the train at Victoria with Kev using loud and fully colourful language as we reviewed the evening's gig. From the seat behind ours emerged a fat, balding middle-aged suited man, on the way home with a suspiciously young woman whose interactions with the guy suggested that she was probably not family, presumably looking to impress her in some strange way. "I don't like your fucking language young man" he offered helpfully, prompting the somewhat obvious reply "Well yours isn't any fucking better mate." I didn't catch sight of the fist, but I remember the fat gold ring on his middle finger that opened my right eye up as it connected flashing in front of me a split second before I was rocked back against the door and blood gushed out. The British Transport Police dragged him from the train whilst his glamorous assistant protested his innocence, and we spent a couple of hours giving statements whilst I was given a tissue or two to stem the flow. Ultimately PC Robb (I have no idea how I remember his name, but I do) advised with fairly obvious dryness that "You know how it's gonna look lads, two youngsters out drinking illegally against the word of a respectable businessman." Despite the fact that my eye was now the size of a rugby ball and the colour of an overripe aubergine, he had a point, and we cut our losses and caught the last train south.

At the time, my father's job had shifted to Milton Keynes, following the fire at Alexandra Palace where he had been based for a few years that finally caused the BBC to leave that fine building for the last time. As a result, he was travelling up there during the week and returning at weekends, so it was only my mum who was at home when I stumbled in at three or four in the morning, which enabled me to seek the motherly nursing I was now craving without having to feel guilty about waking my dad up a couple of hours before he rose for his daily commute. Why I thought this was any fairer on my mum I don't know, but mums are mums and I received the care and attention my suddenly vulnerable back to boyhood ego required, with the obvious and time-honoured application of a pack of frozen peas being administered about five hours too late. A trip to the doctors, a scan in the local hospital, and a headache that lasted for weeks followed, but there was no lasting damage other than that to my pride, and a salutary lesson was learnt. Frustratingly, I had passed my driving test the very morning of that second gig, and my newfound freedom had to be postponed for several weeks as I regained my ability to see anything in singular.

I suspect we were lucky that our brushes with trouble were few and far between. Our single-minded determination to state clearly and loudly our dogged allegiance to our chosen channel of youth culture, our still relatively naïve suburban background coupled with our sometimes lack of plain sensible streetwise nous, and the constant backdrop of violence that accompanied the times were a potentially dangerous mix.

It's a time-spanning parental cliché that's right up there alongside "All your music sounds the same" when discussing what life was like as a teenager in the 70s and early 80s. However, I'm still normally met with dismissive blank looks when I try to explain to today's generation the rigidity and defence of the tribal divisions that existed back then based purely on what sort of music you liked and how you chose to dress as a result. Today's youth have many issues of their own to contend with of course, but the homogenised nature of fashion stylings and level playing field of social media (whatever opinion one may have as to what level of intelligence that particular modern curse engenders) have removed the stark barriers that divided us across our chosen factions so obstinately.

Many a long hour was spent discussing, in earnest social debate, how if punks hated teds, and mods hated teds, then punks and mods must get on OK together right? But then we hated the rockers too, and some of them wore black leather jackets, and so did the punks, so that must make punks similar to rockers, so shouldn't we actually hate punks too? Irrespective of any of this was the unspoken but widely accepted truth that any self-respecting hormone-charged male youth in his late teens harboured a secret desire to own a black leather jacket anyway. And then there were skinheads, seemingly related to our mod world because there was a large crossover in some of the constituent parts of the uniform, and their association with the Two-Tone movement, which had sprung from another previous 60s legacy but one that was culturally intertwined with our own.

Except that some of the skinheads professed to hold extreme right-wing views that we fortunately recognised as abhorrent and unacceptable despite our adherence to style rules and constant influence by peer pressure. Bloody hell it was confusing. And the emergence of the New Romantic movement just flipped our heads way past any level of pretending to understand. With hindsight, for the sake of my wardrobe and my ability to continue to walk tall in public, it is perhaps fortunate that The Vapors split up when they did, as their final "Top Of The Pops" performance revealed a terrifying prototype Duran-ic glimpse of how their appearance may have developed had it been allowed to continue.

Nevertheless, our mod allegiance did lead to a few scrapes along the way, the most comical being with a bunch of Rockabillies on the Metropolitan line somewhere in the suburbs one Saturday afternoon. It was during that final Vapors tour in March 1981, and the band were playing at the Hertfordshire College of Further Education, a campus college situated in a place called Aldenham. We understood this to be somewhere in Watford, but in fact it turned out to be several miles from anywhere, set on the edge of greenbelt land adjacent to the M1 motorway.

Like sixteen-year-olds the length and breadth of the country, as adept as we were in the practice of making sure we made convincing eighteen-year-olds when entry to pubs and clubs was required, we were equally as competent when it came to emphasising our juvenility when buying child-priced train tickets. In those days, London Underground had a maximum 10p fare for under-fifteens at weekends for any single tube journey. The obvious way to get to Watford from

Victoria, therefore, was not to make the short tube hop to Euston and the equally short train ride to Watford Junction. Rather, Kev and I elected to negotiate a convoluted 10p tube journey, culminating in a tortuous crawl from Baker Street to Watford's edge of town underground station.

Somewhere along the way, we became vaguely aware of a group of quiffed, creeper-clad lads entering the carriage along with a smattering of gum-chewing girlfriends. As they moved a little closer, we locked into their conversation, which took the form of a confused, amusing, except for the menace it carried, half discussion half argument between themselves about what the two of us actually appeared to be.

"They're definitely mods," opined one of their number, "because one of them's got loafers on."

"Yeah" came the response, albeit slightly questioningly. "But that one's got really short hair and a Fred Perry," offered another of them helpfully, "so I reckon they're definitely skinheads."

Not unlike the episode of "Blackadder" in which an imprisoned Edmund wrestles with the translation of a tormenting Spanish inquisitor's exaggerated diatribe, only to discover that he would have his testicles sliced off and roasted over a fire if he admitted his allegiance to Satan, or alternatively be hung upside down in a warm vat of marmalade before suffering the same fate if he denied such loyalty, we listened intently to the ongoing debate. Finally, unable to decide whether we were mods or skinheads they decided they were going to have to give us a clump anyway. Fortunately, their weapon of choice was one of the girlfriends' supermarket carrier bags, which felt like it probably contained only a packet of soft cheese and maybe some medium-sized overripe fruit as it was whacked into each of our faces a couple of times, rather than Blackadder's torturer's scythe. "All you had to do was ask!" was the only thought other than bewildered amusement that I remember mustering, as one of them swung a punch that missed by miles catching him off balance and sending him pirouetting through the open doors onto the platform at Harrow-On-The-Hill. His cohorts joined him, the doors shut, and we glided away to safety. An equally bemused elderly man in a flat cap asked if we were OK. We confirmed that we were and in no time had arrived at Watford tube station.

Meeting up with Colin in the depths of Watford's own suburbs, we addressed the potentially thorny issue of negotiating early 80s style local bus services, finally and slightly miraculously finding the college site, and once in its virtually deserted environs, locating the student union bar, where we met Julie and Sarah, and where the band had just arrived. The five of us happened that night to meet Suzanne and her friend Melissa for the first time, who had travelled over from Cambridge for their first Vapors gig and formed with Sarah and Julie the crack glove-puppet wearing outfit that appeared regularly for the rest of the tour.

Violence between rival factions within the same audience was also an unpleasant and all too common feature of the age, and something we experienced twice at Specials gigs, a band for whom this nuisance seemed to be a constant problem at the time, both at the Brighton Top Rank Suite. Inside the venue, fighting was relatively easy to separate oneself from, but the train journey back from the "More Specials" show in the autumn of 1980 found us caught up in some altogether more serious, and dangerous, disorder. The train had only just pulled out of Brighton Station when a couple of blood-soaked youths ran through our carriage, fleeing a group of contorted faced, booted up to the ankles, obscenity yelling skinheads giving chase. As the train pulled into Preston Park, barely two minutes up the line, it was met by a significant number of police officers in what with hindsight must have been an operationally efficient well-timed intervention into an already understood and escalating incident. Although their appearance was reassuring, their first action was not, as it was to invoke some central locking mechanism that none of us were ever aware of having existed on those boneshaking old slam door trains, confining us amongst the carnage and its apparent instigators.

Finding ourselves imprisoned with seriously injured victims and snarling mobs of patrolling skins, we were terrified to feel the glazy stare of a couple of their number fixate on us as we sat frozen in our seats. Our salvation appeared in the most unlikely of forms, with the sudden appearance of a guy we knew vaguely from college, of whom the only real knowledge we had was that he was a member of the same church group as a handful of some of our classmates. That night, however, he was dressed in a Selecter t-shirt and red-laced Doctor Marten boots and he materialised from nowhere and casually informed our potential tormentors that "These two are OK." To this day we have no idea how our impromptu guardian angel had any association with such a clearly unpleasant bunch of individuals, but we made the point of seeking him out later that week to offer our relieved thanks. Before long the police boarded the train, and with precision and efficiency removed what was obviously a targeted, and known to them, group of perpetrators, and soon we were on our way home to the safety of Haywards Heath.

Aside from the sheer ludicrousness of the New Romantic movement having the effect of leaving me largely in despair about the direction of fashion and allowing me to settle into a life of comfort in trainers, jeans and T-shirts, its emergence seemed also to have the more positive effect of dampening the flames of the subdivisions of mainstream youth culture. There are still vast problems today, of course, some of them still attaching themselves unwantedly to various music scene cultures both here and in the US, but as a sweeping generalisation, these are related to the underlying gang culture, that from a purely selfish and dismissive viewpoint exists far away from the parts of popular culture with which I still engage.

Thirty-Five Year Interval

Throughout our eighteen months of teenage Vapors obsessiveness, it had been Steve and Ed that we had got to know best and whose company we enjoyed frequently at both Vapors gigs and other gigs. We'd met Dave and Howard at many of the band's shows, and both were never anything other than friendly, but we never really got to know them that well. In Dave's case this felt, to our immature selves, in some way due to the aura that surrounded him as he became the band's star face, his shoulder length jet black hair and piercing stare becoming a public facing image once "Turning Japanese" began to lead to ever more television appearances. Branka recalls how, years before she met Dave, her scornful father, who clearly didn't make the same effort as my mother had done to put on the pretence of being interested in whatever nonsense their offspring were watching, observed Dave's first "Top Of The Pops" performance. He watched in silence before exclaiming in the scathing way that only a deep Yorkshire accent can properly convey "That one looks like bloody Frankenstein for Christ's sake."

I guess he meant Frankenstein's monster, but that would be splitting hairs, the point was that Dave did have the look and slightly unapproachable coolness of a proper rock star.

We'd often meet Ed and Steve before shows or post soundcheck, just relaxing in the bar area of venues such as

The Marquee. Dave could often be seen nearby, concentration wrapped in isolation completely into the Asteroids machine or whatever state of the art arcade game that the establishment in question had installed.

We'd always say hello, and he'd always say hello back, but the fact was, as Colin recalls eruditely, "He scared the shit out of us."

Dave, who these days I count as a friend both within the context of the band and away from it, with whom it is easy to converse in a relaxed, sociable and intelligent way, finds this hugely amusing. The simple truth is that he has a somewhat shy nature and that he is ten years older than me, which when you're sixteen makes a big difference. In your fifties and sixties that makes a considerably smaller difference, but there was one other factor at play back then that we would never have comprehended in our unempathetic younger years, and that was that Dave's seeming aloofness was down to his significant, pre-show especially, nervousness.

"It's always been the case, and it's never really gone away." he says. "I remember the first night of the 'Setting Sons' tour in Manchester. I woke up that morning and just shook. I shook all day. When we did The Rainbow on that tour my legs wouldn't stop shaking. Physically I couldn't control that." Tellingly, whilst still on the subject of that Rainbow gig, he expresses surprise that the live version of "Here Comes The Judge", recorded that night and which ended up on the B-side of "Turning Japanese", ever made it to release "given how badly I played it." In fact, the 6 minutes 35 seconds, captured for posterity that evening early on in the band's career, is regarded by Vapors fans as a classic, remaining a live favourite staple set-closer to this day, so the version that initially kindled that enthusiasm can't have been too bad. To be fair, Steve backs up Dave's critical assertion. "The last chord of that is shambolic!" he chuckles. "I always try and recreate that when we play it now, do it wrong, but that's more difficult than doing it right!"

But the attention to detail sums Dave's attitude up perfectly. He is determined, obsessively so, to perform at 100% on every occasion, his rationale being that he's a professional, being paid to do what he does, and he cannot at any point afford to let fans or wider potential audience down. The problem for Dave is that, aligned to his overall character, this leads to a fear of failure that manifests itself in pre-show nerves, which begin days before each and every performance. We've had several near arguments over this, as I insist to him that for the majority of the regular fans it's still enough that the band are turning up and playing for us, and that if they were a bit rubbish now and then it wouldn't really matter. But his insistence that if it's worth doing, it's worth doing properly is, in truth, admirable and clearly the right approach, even though, unavoidably as it does, it leads to an anxious few hours or days for him before each show. I've put it to Dave that I wonder whether this is simply a by-product of the band's long ago sudden and rapid rise, which afforded him no opportunity to develop performance experience in a more structured way. He refutes this theory, however, stating that the problem has never really gone away, and if it hasn't done yet, it's not likely to.

The process is, these days, personally managed for him by his wife, who explains that they've built a fairly regular pre-gig routine now, which will involve her getting Dave to recite lyrics, coaxing out of him one of his fears, namely that he'll just forget the songs when he's on stage. He concedes that this is still a problem however, "The new songs, fuck me!" he smiles, at which Branka laughs and says "I just rein him in and say 'look love, it's a question of doing nothing, because you're retired, or doing something you absolutely bloody love' and we always get there." Nevertheless, the nervousness often stays with him throughout the duration of the show, only relaxing when he feels like "We're in total control of it" which, coupled with that obsessive requirement for perfection, doesn't always feel the case to Dave even though everyone else in the hall might be of the opinion that they haven't really put a foot wrong all night.

Dave's involvement with Branka, and one assumes therefore the trust and understanding that has built up over a long marriage and presumably accounts for the way she is able to help at a personal level now that he has returned to regular gigging, stems back to not long after The Vapors had split up. Having had a taste of success in the music business, he allied himself to that lifestyle rather than plot an immediate return to the conventions of legal practice. Initially he took a job as a sound engineer at The Cartoon Club in Croydon where he worked for a good six years or so, during which time he released his only solo single "Fresh Air" in 1983, a record with a slightly more electronic, quite possibly Devo-influenced early 80s vibe to it than The Vapors records had carried.

Branka had completed "A" levels in Leeds and turned her attention to finding appropriate higher education. "I was supposed to go to Middlesex Poly to do a course in

Performance Art", she remembers. All set, her Yorkshire-via-Serbia father intervened.

It would seem he didn't hold back. "What the bloody hell are you going to do there?" he reasoned. "Why don't you do a business degree?"

"Well dad I've got to go Middlesex, I can't..."

"No, we'll find you somewhere else."

So a place was found on her behalf at Croydon College in Business Studies. "Alright dad. I'll do that to keep you happy" was apparently her straightforward response, suggesting that maybe some of the good-natured stubbornness that seems to be a fairly major part of her character had yet to develop.

"So I went down South, one of my friends said, 'Oh we know this girl down there who's in a band, they're looking for a singer.'" And on her first day in Croydon she thought "Yeah I'll do it."

She performed "House Of The Rising Sun" at the band audition ("it was shite, but I got in!") and recollects in a slightly amazed but undoubtedly delighted way, "And we did ok! We went to Stonehenge, we played the last festival there in 1984, it was great!"

"And then one day our manager said 'Right, I'm bringing this guy into rehearsal, he's from a famous band!' and I'm like yeah, cool, famous band, great, bring him in!"

At this point in the recounting of the story, Branka begins to laugh uncontrollably before recovering and continuing whilst still trying to hold back the guffaws, "I'm sorry, but I thought he was Charlie Harper!" She continues the laughter. "So Dave came down", turning to him as she recalls her first meeting with the famous guy, ten years her senior, "and I think I kicked you, didn't I?"

"Yeah," he confirms with the amused but accepting shrug he has probably had to pull out several thousand times subsequent to that first encounter.

"'Who the fuck are you?' I asked." Branka continues, still chuckling over her words before concluding with the fairly obvious statement that "He so wasn't Charlie Harper."

My mind briefly ran through a bizarre "Back To The Future" style stretch of the imagination that had me picturing what may have developed musically if he had actually been the legendary punk and blues musician, himself ten years' Dave's senior, and what bizarre direction the UK Subs may have taken as a consequence, before Branka manages to stifle the giggles and continues.

"So he came down to rehearsal, and he quite liked our stuff, and he said, 'would you like to be in a band with me?' And I said yeah, but I've got all of these people around me." Drawing another accepting shrug she puts it to Dave that "I think you just pissed everyone else off didn't you?"

"Yeah" he returns again, this time expanding on the story a little, explaining "Yeah, it was the idea of having a second drummer that they didn't like. Especially the drummer."

Dave got a second drummer in.

"My band went to shit when Dave came along. Anyway, I lost them, and I found him. Awesome really!"

Somewhere along the way, they became a couple, and a new band, The Vapor Corporation, was formed, built around the pair.

Dave wrote lyrics for Branka to sing, describing how he enjoyed the different writing perspective. "It was fantastic for me, writing from a third person's point of view. That was really enjoyable. I did perform with them sometimes, but I didn't have to play."

"I'd always wanted to be a songwriter more than a musician. If I found someone that could play it for me, I wouldn't do it, I don't necessarily want to be doing that. My love is writing songs, not playing them," he continues, before somewhat belying that claim with the qualification that "even still, though, I wanted to make another album of music."

Branka's brother joined the group, along with others, with drummers coming and going, Michael Bowes eventually taking up the role.

Following school and a year at college, Michael had begun an apprenticeship with British Caledonian Airways at Gatwick Airport. With a dismissive statement that doesn't quite convey the impressiveness of its content he explains that "I just kind of did quite well and moved up through the company. I became an aircraft designer." But for all that his love of aeroplanes was being fed by his professional work, his love of drumming was continuing apace in the background playing in reggae bands, before diversifying into soul and funk and more rockier sounds as time went by as a result of playing with a born again Christian Rock band in Crawley. They in turn persuaded him to play songs far, far removed from his reggae roots including Yes and Genesis numbers. He'd moved down to Crawley to be near his work but would still return to a spiritual home in Croydon, the instrument and equipment shop Rockbottom Music, because it "had always been my music store." He knew many staff and customers alike and found himself chatting one day to a member of Branka's band who mentioned that they were looking for a drummer. "The last band I had worked with, they kind of fell apart after we had finished backing Desmond Dekker" he throws in equally as casually, so he auditioned for The Vapor Corporation and took up the role. "I only stayed for a year or so, though, because the guitarist left the band to form a power trio and I went to play with him because by that time I'd gone full on metal", he grins.

The Vapor Corporation struggled to find a guitarist, finally advertising in Melody Maker. "We ran auditions. It was so grim. Everyone was shit, but then we got something in the post from a guy in Germany called Michael Stephens. He was American, he was a rock and roll victim, imagine Steven Tyler on speed with a 'flying V' guitar."

He flew over and auditioned with the band and got the job. He had nowhere to stay in London so Branka and Dave invited him back to theirs for the night, where he stayed for six months.

It was a fraught six months, but the enigmatic guitarist was able to use connections to get gigs, with the band playing in well-established London pubs and clubs including the Sir George Robey in Finsbury Park, The Bull and Gate in Kentish Town and The Rock Garden in the heart of the Covent Garden piazza, none of them still in existence as music venues.

The band's story ended soon after. The end is described with a sweeping arm and the unconcerned explanation that "It just all went pear shaped really", followed by the simple yet clearly fairly momentous statement that "Then we got married and had kids."

Family life, mortgages, two sons and a daughter necessitated a regular income, and the bits of paper that Dave had taken such care to assemble prior to the musician's life were pulled from the bottom drawer. In the 90s Dave became the in-house lawyer for the Musicians' Union, combining the qualifications with his on-the-job experience of the music industry and, just as he never regretted the shot at the music world, he looks back on his subsequent career with an equal pride and enthusiasm. "It was interesting, and I was helping people" he reasons. "I got bigger and better at it than anything I'd done in the music. If I was going to have to earn money, it wasn't a bad thing to do."

The family settled in Hertfordshire, Dave commuted into London, the children grew up, and in 2016 Dave was to retire, with the family moving to the South Coast a couple of years later. But he still hadn't made that third album.

Ed's subsequent film school training and graduation led to an equally long and successful career as that which Dave's bits of paper had given him.

Education complete, Ed embarked on a successful, diverse career that is very much still in full swing to this day. His early professional work involved sound engineering for BBC productions, with credits stretching back to the early 90s and including Dubbing Editor work for series such as "Campion" and "Lovejoy". His efforts began to be recognised quite early on, with a BAFTA TV award nomination for his sound work on "Middlemarch" in 1995 and for his editing work on an edition of "Airport" made the following year.

Gradually, the shift to production and direction was made, where it remains full steam ahead, and he is perhaps best known for his directorial work on episodes of "Doctor Who" and "Poldark", and another BAFTA TV award nominated work, an episode of 2003's "Seven Wonders of the Industrial World" documentary series that focuses on the work of his great-great-grandfather Joseph Bazalgette, who designed and engineered London's Victorian sewer network. The catalogue of Ed's other work is long and varied, however, and includes Director credits for various episodes of mainstream TV staples such as "Casualty", "Holby City" and "Top Gear".

Steve, meanwhile, continued in the industry, playing in a succession of bands, becoming a well-respected sound engineer, and interspersing the technical aspects with the performing aspects throughout the rest of his working life, continuing in the same vein today.

"I carried on with the playing until about 1986 though", he says. Shoot! Dispute recorded some Peel sessions and played the circuit for a while, releasing a single, and supporting Bruce Foxton on his own post-Jam solo tour. In the mid-80s, the work balance switched from performing to sound engineering, which became the primary money-earner for Steve, although he never stopped playing in any number of guises.

"I think it was 1984 or 1985." Steve looks back when he describes meeting Dunc (Du Kane), who was, in due course, effectively to become Steve's longest-lasting ever bandmate. "Dunc asked me to produce a demo for him and he became one of my best mates." Du Kane himself is best known for his 90s project Beautiful People, essentially a post-rave explosion techno band.

They remained friends, with Steve continuing, captivated in what he's describing, "He did a Hendrix sample album; this was in the 90s. He put a Hendrix track to dance music, people liked it, someone gave it to Clapton, Clapton gave it to Alan Douglas, the keeper of the Hendrix estate and he contacted Dunc to make a whole album of it! Incredible!"

They lost touch for a while, but when Steve dreamed up the idea for The Shakespearos, something which he is clearly proud of, and was very much his own project, "The first person I contacted was Dunc." They've now been playing in the band together for the best part of a decade.

Following his work for the PRS, and his input helping compile (and create sleeve notes for) a Vapors CD compilation that was released by EMI, Howard opened a small independent record store in Guildford named People Records, finally closing it in early 2016 after making another conscious decision, after the lease expired, to devote to family time following the arrival of his new born son the previous October. He had also remained active behind the scenes in Guildford promoting local gigs, and perhaps more impressively given that he'd undoubtedly be swimming against the tide in that part of Surrey, getting involved with politics and standing as the Labour Party candidate for Guildford in the 2017 General Election.

Michael Bowes, meanwhile, had found his career going from strength to strength, transferring to British Airways to work as part of the aircraft design team that worked on Concorde, before eventually deciding to go freelance in an attempt for once and for all to concentrate in a more focussed way on the drumming. He combined contract work for BA and Virgin Atlantic Airways with trying to earn money playing both live and as a session musician, and his break came when he was playing in a funk band named The Blunter Brothers, who performed James Brown and Stevie Wonder covers amongst other numbers. "Richard Branson would host these huge parties on his estate for staff from all of his businesses" he explains. "In those days that included Virgin Records, so you'd get all the stars there, he'd lay on food and drink and bands and hold a whole series of these across a few weekends in the summer. And then one time he booked The Blunter Brothers!" Not only did it feel like a big occasion, but equally importantly he finally got to play to his colleagues, workmates and bosses who were forced to pay attention and in his words "finally realised what I had been going on about at work all the time, that I could actually play!" Arrangements were made to formally reduce his working days to two a week, and he set about ramping up his "Michael Bowes Music" business.

The CV from that point on is impressive, with Michael having played with a huge portfolio of acts. Diverse doesn't begin to cover it, with the pop side of his work including performances with hugely respected acts such as Tears For Fears, as well as "EastEnders" stars turned pop stars Sid Owen and Michelle Gayle. Nelly Furtado, Heather Small and Joss Stone, with whom he has also written, all feature on his list. Reggae has still been represented with work with Bass Culture, as has progressive rock with Moondigger, and even comedy has had its part with a stint as Stephen K Amos's house band drummer for a run at the Hammersmith Apollo.

As the music took off, the aircraft career finally had to make a soft landing and these days, having also obtained teaching qualifications, Michael works part time (around the drumming as best he can) in a Further Education role allied closely to his musical skills in Brighton.

Back across the Atlantic, in the intervening period, Evan Blonder had graduated, and taken up a veterinarian's post in New Jersey where a customer wandered in one day with a suffering beagle and noticed Evan's ever-present Beatles button badge. They got talking, and it turned out that the guy was an equally big Beatles fan and was a guitarist with local musical connections and who was friends with Blondie drummer Clem Burke, who grew up locally. The two of them chatted, became friends and would play songs regularly with the guy, who had his own Beatles cover band.

Evan moved to Long Island where he set up his own business, got married, had children, and had to put the guitar away for a while, but continued to wear the trusty Beatles badge. Early this century the playing was resurrected when a couple brought in their stricken Jack Russell terrier and he was invited over to their house to see the woman's Beatles collection, once again as a result of the small circular fan statement worn on his lapel. But she also played guitar, and they jammed together a bit, Evan contacted a bassist he knew, who in turned called up a drummer, and all of a sudden, they had a band. The Beagles spent the next few years performing Beatles covers around the area, and after they stopped playing Evan continued to play with friends' bands on a semi-regular basis. Following the subsequent history of ex-Beatles members' lives and the ongoing careers of those still with us is, of course, relatively easy to do, but like so many of us he spent decades wondering what had become of the former Vapors, still the band that was number 2 in his heart.

Likewise, up in Woodstock, New York, Bobby Weiss was playing in bands when the day job allowed, always harbouring a curiosity as to the whereabouts of the members of the group that he credits for the very fact that he became a participatory musician in the first place.

Mid-way through the 90s, Dave's second son Dan was born. Unsurprisingly, Dan tells how the question he most has to answer in life is "What was it like growing up as Dave Fenton's son?" His answer is relatively straightforward, and equally as obvious: "Just like growing up with any other family in Harpenden really. Dad was working in London or at home, Jack (his older brother) and Lana (his younger sister) and me went to school, mum and dad looked after us and it was a comfortable, happy childhood."

Dan's earliest musical memories are, on paper at least, slightly less remarkable than his father's had been, the first album he remembers owning being a Busted album that an aunt bought for him. "Never mind Blur v Oasis," he laughs, "it was Busted versus McFly that was really important when I was 8!" He did, however, have that same luxury as his dad had been afforded all those years before, an older brother with a record collection, and he soon set Dan on the path to the music that still lights his fire the most as he moves into his mid-twenties. "Jack came home from HMV one day and I heard this operatic, screamy heavy guitar noise, and these banging drums emitting from his bedroom door," he enthuses. "He'd gone out and bought 'The Number Of The Beast' by Iron Maiden and I just kind of thought 'I like the sound of that!'"

Through Jack, he got into a lot of other metal bands; The Darkness, Guns n' Roses and lots more Iron Maiden formed his soundtrack when he was just 10 and 11. He struck up a friendship at school with a boy with similar tastes, and they would make regular as clockwork fortnightly trips to HMV to spend their combined pocket money on shared ownership CDs before going home and spending the next two weeks listening to them together. "We buried our heads in the past whilst schoolmates were into all of the current commercial stuff", he remembers with pride.

Despite their musical pasts, his parents never tried to push him into music, but at the age of 12 Dave bought him a half-sized acoustic guitar and taught him two chords (E minor and G, he recalls with an impressive sense of accuracy) and this turned out to be the only guitar training he ever received, everything else he learnt being self-taught. He had always known that his father had once been a musician, and was even aware that there were some CDs on the shelf bearing his name and that of his band, but he credits his sister for cracking them out and playing them, allowing him to listen to them for the first time at an age when his musical tastes and knowledge had developed to enough of a degree to appreciate what he was listening to. "I just thought it was brilliant" says Dan, recycling the joy we'd all felt nearly 30 years previously, but it must have been a little different knowing that the singer and songwriter of what you are discovering for the first time is your own father.

"It took me a while to even find out that there was such a thing as live music though", he continues. "I thought CDs were all there were! But one day a friend's mum bought tickets for me and my mate to go and see a band." He hesitates while I probe him for more information before coyly explaining that "It was Kid Creole and the Coconuts."

He adds, unnecessarily, "In St Albans" as if that would somehow make it OK, but I guess at least it wasn't Busted. It wasn't exactly The Beatles either though. His mum set him on the path to recovery and to an understanding of what live versions of the sort of music he was now loving could be like, buying the two brothers tickets for an AC/DC concert in 2009.

All the while, he continued to mess around with his half-sized acoustic guitar, playing along to songs, learning chords, finding his way up and down the strings and the fretboard, until a year later his CD playing mate became the proud owner of a Squier Stratocaster complete with a 5W Marshall amp. "I went round and I played it and I was like 'this is cool'" he states simply. "So I got one for Christmas. The first riff I played on it was 'Turning Japanese.'"

All the while, he was falling more in love with music, and more in love with playing, sitting in front of his CD player and just playing along to anything and everything, improvising his own parts, and just seeing where it took him, still with no training. "I had to Google how to hold a plectrum after a while," he laughs, "as I'd been doing it wrong for two years and wondered why I couldn't get the downstrokes to work at all!"

He can't remember at what point he learned to play The Vapors songs but explains straightforwardly that "I liked them. And if I like something, I learn to play it."

As he got older, he says that he became more and more aware of just how many people knew of, and liked, his father's music. "So me and mum started pestering him a good few years back now, 'Go on dad, get the band back together!' But he never really showed that much interest."

I Got No Idea Where I Go From Here

Meanwhile, back in the suburban South East, post-Vapors and post-Chords world, but with ever increasing amounts of money earnt from trekking as many miles of the Haywards Heath hinterlands as I could possibly cover, shoving endless leaflets of the sort that are immediately discarded by every household that ever finds them dropping through the letter box, I fed my gig habit. The Brighton scene was strong, both in the pubs and in the larger venues with regular shows from established touring bands, and trips to London were frequent to see bands like White Heat, who we'd grown to love on that last Vapors tour, The Gymslips, who became the latest in my list of "can't miss" bands playing regularly on the smaller London pub and club circuit, and whatever bands were left at the tail end of the rapidly shrinking mod revival movement.

Gigs were interspersed with "A" levels and in 1982 these were duly attained, shortly after which my parents upped roots and moved to Leighton Buzzard, a Haywards Heath clone tucked exactly the same distance to the north of London as Haywards Heath was to the south. Although the Bedfordshire town had a more historic centre than the post-railway concrete of my home since childhood, it proved to be even duller. It had been chosen for practicalities, with my father's job now permanently settled in Milton Keynes.

Somehow or other, despite my early obsession with music, and an equally early discovery of pubs and more importantly being able to get served in them from the age of about fifteen onwards, I had still managed to conduct myself diligently through a relatively high achievement schooling, and "A" levels were successfully negotiated. Careers advice, set in the heart of the accountancy and city commuting dormitory population and still driven by the school's previous grammar school background was, however, singularly uninspiring. I remember being informed, with an assumption that I would be hugely excited at the prospect, that I should consider developing a career as an actuary. I had no idea then what one of them was, and I have very little idea now. The plotting of my rosy future was somewhat confused for me when, during the very same conversation, the very same careers counsellor followed this suggestion with a casual "Or what about becoming a primary school teacher?"

What was clearer in terms of the roadmap the school had already plotted for me without seemingly placing any importance about understanding the person that I was actually growing up to be, was that they felt with my academic ability and potential I should consider applying for an Oxbridge place. Although thoughts had turned to University by that point, I did at least know that this was just simply not an option. I was self-aware enough by seventeen to reason that the academic pantomime that would accompany such a higher education just wouldn't cut it for me. I also had the strong suspicion that the wonderful world of Oxford or Cambridge was being sold to me not for my benefit, but for the school's benefit, as it would represent another notch on the archaic honours boards that hung on the main hall's walls.

Besides, there was only one place I wanted to live by that point, and that was palpably Central London, preferably within walking distance of my now beloved music venues.

There was undoubtedly some scouring of prospectuses in at least a token attempt to match a course to my abilities, and even maybe interest, but my choice of college was driven by a simple methodology. I looked up the addresses of pretty much every hall of residence associated with every college affiliated to the University of London and mapped them out in an A to Z guidebook. University College London was chosen with very little attention to any minutiae-like detail such as what studying there may involve, but around the sound logic that I could get accommodation through them in the heart of Camden Town.

I took a year off before University, my father managing to talk the BBC into taking me on in their Milton Keynes studios. I earnt some money and I spent the money, but I met a lot of real people of the sort I never associated with during my sheltered schooling, and I genuinely loved every minute of it. I became good mates with the second of three regular gig-going buddies named Kev in my life, a chef from the BBC canteen, and we'd regularly travel down to Euston after work to see bands in London. The Alarm became our go-to band of choice, their stealth arrival in my world having worn me into submission. I first saw them, slightly incongruously, supporting The Beat, thinking that the acoustic guitar slinging, harmonica toting, punk posturing from the guy with the silly hair was a bit weird, and then shortly afterwards they turned up again supporting U2 at The

Lyceum. By the time, a couple of months later, that they opened for Stiff Little Fingers, I reached the conclusion that I wasn't going to be able to shake them off, and they became a regular, Marquee playing, sweat generating favourite for both of the Kevs and myself.

The year passed and I moved into Camden Town. Living there, and in London in general, was everything I had hoped it would be, and more. I was within five minutes' walk of Camden High Street and Camden Lock, a bus ride from the West End, a bus ride from the Arsenal ground and a quick tube ride across town to get to see Sarah in Streatham, our Roehampton differences having long since been settled, or to the music venues in Hammersmith, or anywhere else I bloody well wanted. It was truly fantastic. The only downside was the college bit. In my keenness to avoid the prehistoric academia of Oxbridge, I had neglected to factor in that large parts of London University, my own college included, were still stuck in what were to me, totally alien traditions wrapped in incomprehensible language that I neither understood nor connected with in any way. I had spent a year surrounded almost entirely, for the first time, by people I identified with, rather than friends I had to handpick from a large selection, but during college hours in that first year, it felt like a very big socially backwards step.

I somehow scraped through the first year, and moved slightly north into a cold, tatty, damp and miserable house in Avenell Road, Highbury, for the second year. Despite ticking all of the student house cliché boxes, it was again perfect, being less than two minutes' walk from the Piccadilly Line, and directly over the road from the turnstiles leading into the

North Bank of Arsenal Stadium. Many times that year I crawled out of bed at five to three but still made kick-off.

Inevitably the education suffered; I loved everything about London, except the main reason that I was supposed to be there, so I simply stopped bothering with it.

The predictable second year failure followed, and I moved back to Leighton Buzzard for the summer and got another three-month contract at the BBC, but somehow or other I knew I had to get back to London. Three months of sleeping on friends' floors and sofas followed. I met my future wife and became an instant hit with her parents who thrived at dinner parties in their middle-class environs of Cambridge with tales of how their daughter was dating an unemployed homeless man. Eventually dole money and housing benefit combined to somehow permit the renting of a tiny one and a bit bedroom flat on the Camden Road, with myself having the bit, and Dave Clark, a college friend who had applied himself more diligently and was in his third year, having the bedroom. Dave became a flatmate for many years and remains a good friend and gig buddy to this day.

Spending power became an issue again, so after days trawling Evening Standard ads and hand-written cards in Holloway Job Centre I pulled one of them from its mounting, slung it at the bloke at the counter and said, "I reckon I can do this." I don't remember much of the conversation, or indeed the subsequent job interview, but I ended up working in an office on the Old Street Roundabout ordering, despatching and generally managing spare parts for Philips Business Systems, the nascent computing arm of the Dutch electronics giant. The job was good, the company was good, the pay was good, my habits were funded. After a couple of years, I was asked into the manager's office.

Brian Jones didn't change my life, but in five short minutes he played a significant part in shaping a large part of the remainder, at least thus far.

"Sit yourself down, I just wanted a chat really." He waved vaguely at the state of the art ostentatiously 1980s office chair, all levers and leather padding. I obliged, trying to look confident and relaxed, but brimming with nervous curiosity as to why I had been summoned to the boss's office.

BJ (his rather obvious nickname) was a corpulent, balding, affable, moustachioed cliché of a middle manager. As someone whose only perception of office life up until two years previously had been gleaned through television comedy and drama, I couldn't help but compare him to his near namesake, CJ from the "Reginald Perrin" series. But, despite his hackneyed office layout with its curved, sweeping, oversized wooden desk, its statement-of-intent big phone (with more buttons than could feasibly be programmed), its late Jurassic-era word processor and its multi-storey car park of a paper tray, BJ was no CJ. He was a considerate and effective manager, whose stewardship of the London branch had resulted in happy customers supported by a loyal, contented workforce.

"HR have asked me to have a word" he began, slightly ominously. "They feel that whilst you're doing a great job, you are perhaps, well, a little overqualified for the position." The immediate jolt of anxiety that the opening statement had caused was quickly reversed as he continued with a smile and what almost looked like a wink, "So rather than lose you, we were wondering if there was anything you'd seen within the organisation that may interest you in terms of career progression?"

It was a direct question, to which I responded with a direct question of my own, stacked with intent. "Those engineers, the ones I hand the spare parts out to every day, they get company cars with the job, is that right?"

"Yep," came the matter of fact response, "but if you wanted to go down that route, you'd need to complete a six-week training course. Just outside Amsterdam."

So here I was, a carefree 23-year-old, seemingly being offered a fully expensed month and a half in a city that was very much on my to-do list, at the end of which I would be furnished with a free car and a substantial pay rise. In modern parlance, it was a no-brainer. I asked BJ as calmly as I could, "So how soon would that be able to be arranged?"

"Well, we'd need to check your aptitude for the job," he opined unconcernedly, "but as I believe you hold Maths and Physics "A" levels you've nothing to worry about there, you're perfectly qualified."

The conversation was brief, and I left the room elated. The extra money, the travel, the status, that company car, they all felt good, but in reality, what Brian Jones had done was set me on the road to what became a long and successful professional career. The end product would be the same as the one lazily assumed for me back at my out-of-touch school, one of a successful working life, a wonderful family, a comfortable and no less wonderful existence, built around a rich and varied livelihood earned as an IT consultant that started the minute he closed the door on that meeting. But the route I took to get there had not been the one presumed for me by the aspirational one-dimensional stereotyping of my 1970s schooling.

I don't necessarily regard the two-year stint at University as a waste of time. With hindsight I wouldn't have bothered, but it didn't really matter once I'd started working, was living where I wanted, was earning good money in a good job, and felt completely in control.

Over the next few weeks, months and years, I completed that initial training, and more. I found myself in the right place at the right time in the burgeoning computer industry, and I never looked back. For the first two or three years, BJ was omnipresent; encouraging, motivating, supporting and always there to provide advice. These days, he'd be referred to as a mentor, or a work coach, or an executive sponsor. Back then, he was just a bloody good boss.

Dave Clark and I moved to a larger flat in Hornsey, Dave's girlfriend moved in, and then out, and then Dave moved out. My girlfriend moved in and the archetypal early twenties shared flatmate lifestyle was replaced with the more ordered, cleaner, slightly later twenties living as a couple lifestyle. Beccy was building a career too, and we took the next logical step and began to look for a flat of our own to buy.

We searched all over Hornsey, Crouch End, Harringay and the surrounding areas to no avail, eventually finding a perfect, if tiny, second floor flat in a Victorian terrace just five minutes from Wood Green tube station. It fitted our requirements, it fitted our price range, public transport was perfect, and we could park outside. There was just one problem for me, and that was having to swallow the bitter pill of the address. We had a serious life chat that lasted several seconds and went something like:

"Are you sure you're ready for this? Taking on a mortgage together is a big commitment for us both."

"Yeah no worries."

"OK then."

And before long I moved into White Hart Lane.

Throughout the late 80s I had almost completely fallen out of love with music. The few bands from the early 80s that remained had become dull and boring, or turned into tedious rock dinosaurs, and try as I did, I could never really embrace the whole rave/dance scene with the same enthusiasm. Coupled with the disposable income and fully funded company car, football took over as obsession number one, and I would regularly travel the length and breadth of the country to support Arsenal. Simon Nicholson, who became my regular football partner in crime for over twenty years was a constant companion, as were other acquaintances who we'd met, and became friends with in The Copenhagen, the Holloway pub that had become my surrogate front room when I had shared that flat in Camden Road with Dave.

So whilst the flat in Wood Green was perfect, it took some mental torture before I accepted that it would be OK to move into a street, at the other end of which, albeit two miles to the east, was the home stadium of the enemy.

The 90s came along, and Beccy and I became friends with a number of locals, largely met in The Nelson, a large pub opposite Wood Green bus garage that was always busy with town centre passing trade and loyal regular locals. I met the third Kev, my age and also an Arsenal fan. We spoke about music, recalling our mutual early love of The Stranglers, the long-gone mayhem and excitement of Jam gigs, and re-tracked our parallel early lives. Kev had grown up in Wood Green and maintained friendships with old schoolmates who lived locally.

He introduced me to Chris, who lived in Bounds Green, had also travelled the same musical journey and lived the full-on mod life in the late 70s. "Yeah I even ran a fanzine," Chris mentioned one evening, "it was called Fightback."

I spluttered into my beer. "Fightback did you say? Did you run it with a guy called Rudi?"

Kev in turn spluttered into his beer before Chris could answer.

"Do you know Rudi?" he asked, eyes incredulous with amazement.

"Well I did back then," I said. "He was friends with my mate Colin."

"Little Colin that worked in the shop?" asked Chris, joining in the incredulity as Kev continued, "Rudi's one of my best mates to this day!"

The extent of our small world established, Kev and Chris, neither of whom, tragically, are still with us, went on to become regular football and gig buddies, despite the fact that at the beginning of the decade I was still struggling to really find anything musically that carried any real level of excitement. That began to change with the emergence of bands like The Stone Roses and The Happy Mondays, who themselves would not have existed if it hadn't been for the evolution of the rave scene of course, but a lot of our in-depth music discussions over beer in the pub were still reflective of older times.

Another serious life chat with Beccy ensued late one night between Christmas and New Year over a chicken jalfrezi in the Wood Green Tandoori when she casually asked, "So what shall we do next year then?"

"Dunno." I responded, assuming she was thinking of summer holidays, "What do you fancy?"

"Well we could get married if you want?" she continued.

Seemed like a plan, so we duly carried it out the following October.

And also in 1993, music was once again saved. And this time, wonder of wonders, it was saved by someone I was soon to learn hailed from my childhood hometown, the place whose importance in my life I had strived so hard to minimise as I cultivated my cool London persona in early adulthood, but a place for which in reality I retained a nostalgic fondness.

I can't recall the exact date, but I know it must have been early spring. I was crawling through the early evening rush hour traffic, daylight fading after a sunny day driving around London fixing state of the art Compaq DeskPro PCs, making weary but contented slow progress along Parkway in Camden Town. In those days, like many other in the know Londoners, my radio station of choice was Greater London Radio, which provided an intelligent cosmopolitan mix of contemporary and classic rock and pop, mixed with largely light-hearted informational programming and talk shows. For some reason on this particular day, however, I had Radio 1's afternoon show playing away unobtrusively in the background, when my attention was caught by a rasping, crashing guitar introduction to a song that led immediately into a stylised, Bowie-esque vocalisation that kicked through the next three minutes underpinned by a swirling guitar hook line and thumping rhythm.

I'd heard of the band, and was aware of some hype being generated around them, but despite my late 80s music-scene apathy having been lifted from rock bottom by that point, I had yet to resume actively seeking out bands and responding to recommendations as I had done over a decade earlier. This song caught me square between the ears at first hearing, however. I cranked up the radio volume and once it was back-announced by Steve Wright and I was able to put two and two together about the identity of the artists, I headed straight to the record shop in Wood Green Shopping City on my way home, and purchased "Animal Nitrate" by Suede.

Suede quickly became a favourite, some of their London gigs remain as strong and as fond memories as a lot from The Jam era, and if I have such a thing "Dog Man Star" is probably my favourite album of all time. Brett Anderson's recent, excellent memoir "Coal Black Mornings" detailing his life up to the point that Suede signed a record deal describes in detail his recollection of growing up in Haywards Heath as a boy four years younger than myself. His childhood and his immediate neighbourhood were very different to mine, but nonetheless his descriptions of the town, most notably in terms of its feel, rather than its appearance, carry strong imagery that resonates very strongly and accurately. I often pass through the town, and it doesn't look to have changed an awful lot. The optimistically named Broadway has become a cosmopolitan gastronomic hub, with a collection of bars and restaurants whose numbers spread close to, or maybe even reach, double figures. South Road remains a fairly typical high street; independent fishmongers, butchers and grocers have been replaced by charity shops, small supermarkets and newsagents by pound shops and coffee-chain cafes, and there is no hint of a record store. But the pedestrian crossings remain modern and conform to the latest standards of advanced crossing technology, with an impressive third one having been added to the glittering array.

The whole 90s music scene rekindled things in full for me, a night at Alexandra Palace seeing Blur with Pulp as support felt as era-defining a moment as some late 70s experiences, not least so for Beccy who, a few months subsequent to our third big life chat, spent the evening beginning to feel the effects of her first pregnancy.

Our first son was born in 1995, and we wrestled with the reality of needing more spacious accommodation, by then a largely unaffordable option in the relatively local parts of North London that we would have preferred to inhabit if we were going to stay in the city to bring kids up. Beccy would quite happily have moved to the country, my rural agoraphobia and equally strong fear of living somewhere that wasn't a short hop from gig venues preventing such an outcome. We settled on Brighton, known to me from childhood, known to Beccy from our ever more frequent weekend drives down to see my sister Jeanette who had already moved there, and perfect for city living and quick escape to countryside in equal measures. After leaving Philips I'd spent a few years working for a growing computer reseller in Islington, and by the time we moved south I'd moved again to work for a services provider in Orpington, Kent. This made the drive to work from the south coast practical, and resulted in hours of motorway bound radio listening with the enthusiasm afforded to the original XFM incarnation, and shows like Radio 1's "Evening Session" coming as close to anything radio had done to excite me since school nights smuggling John Peel under my covers.

My employer promptly went bust, and I ended up having to join the ranks of Southern Railway commuters that I had been so scornful of in my youth, with the added indignity of having to stop at Haywards Heath station on the way to London and back so that the train could load and unload the latest generation of identikit grey suits.

But I enjoyed the work, and with the addition of son number two in 1998 Brighton was a great place to be, suiting all four of us in its various ways. Britpop came and went, and the early years of the millennium were soundtracked more by emerging US bands like Interpol, The Strokes and The White Stripes than UK ones, to varying extents, but the ongoing immersion in music never subsided again in the way that it had done in the 80s.

The growth of the Internet accelerated, and I began to trawl through sites thinking that it was probably high time to rekindle long lost acquaintances. I posted the obligatory entry against my old school on "Friends Reunited" and before long had received a couple of emails from a couple of vaguely remembered friends who I am sure were pleasant enough, but I wasn't finding the people I really wanted to find.

And then one day I received a brief message asking simply "Are you the Mike Philpott from Haywards Heath that was really into The Vapors?"

To my delight, I didn't have to find Colin because he had found me. We chatted, caught up on twenty years of life, agreed we'd have to meet when practical, and I turned my attention to locating Kev number one, with whom I'd also lost touch in the mid-80s.

Kev himself was living and working in Germany and was in turn amusing himself of an evening on the burgeoning world wide web, seeking out music history and references to his own long-lost past. Like I had done, he had come across a website named "Secret Noise" run by Vapors fan Par Engstrom, and familiar to many Vapors fans as the website that kept the flame burning for so long. Unlike me, however, Kev had posted a memory on the site's guestbook page, detailing the long overnight walk back from the last gig at Roehampton to Victoria. Colin had seen the post, realised it must have been made by one of his small hours hiking companions from 25 years ago, and duly got in touch with Kev via the email link he had left on the web page.

Colin accordingly put me and Kev in touch, and Kev rang me on my mobile just as I was boarding a train from Brighton to London one evening for some long-forgotten football match. Coincidentally, he was ringing because he was in the UK visiting his mother, still based in Haywards Heath, and he too was on his way to London for the evening. With a happy, fitting, decade-spanning synchronicity, we co-ordinated time and location, and he stepped onto my train as it pulled into Haywards Heath. We chatted, and chatted, and chatted some more. On arrival at Victoria we headed straight over the road to The Shakespeare and drank and chatted, and drank and chatted, and drank and chatted some more. We could have gone on for days, but regular contact was resumed and whenever Kev was in the UK from that point onwards, we made the point of getting together, often using the occasion to take in an appropriate gig in Brighton if the opportunity presented itself.

We finally got an evening together for all three of us to meet up when Kev was in the country and we were both able to travel to London to meet up with Colin, who caught the train down from Milton Keynes where he had settled with his own family, chatting for hours in a pub at Euston Station.

The conversation was, of course, largely centred around one thing and one thing only, and I recall one particularly wistful and misty-eyed several drinks in moment when Colin offered the view that "Life's good generally, but sometimes I think I'd give anything, just anything, to be able to travel back in time for just one night with you guys, to a Vapors gig at The Marquee or somewhere."

"It'll never happen Col," we sniggered back.

Waiting For The Weekend

Halfway through 2016 I got the call. I was sitting at my desk at home one evening, situated at the rear of the front room, half-heartedly keeping an eye on whatever Beccy was watching on TV, and equally unattentively flicking through news sites on my PC.

"The Vapors are reforming!" yelled Kev down the phone immediately I answered it, before either of us had exchanged any traditional phone-call conversation openers.

I don't recall my immediate response, but I do remember then leaping from my seat and yelling the same phrase back down the phone uncontrollably several times at the top of my voice whilst feeling like (and I imagine acting like) a ten year old boy getting the racing bike he'd always craved on his birthday (or whatever the modern day equivalent is). Wryly amused by her husband's sudden man-child behaviour, my wife opined that "They'll have to halve the venue capacity to accommodate all the beer guts", before showing a little more interest as I quizzed Kev as to what he knew. Very little, it turned out, but Colin had messaged him to say that he'd seen it on Facebook, and it was definitely for real. We made excited commitments to travel to the first gig, wherever it may be, which didn't feel like too big a deal for me as we assumed it would be in either Guildford or London but was more so for Kev who was living in Frankfurt.

Despite (or maybe because of) a lifetime in Information Technology, I had, until 2016, resolutely and stubbornly resisted Social Media (an achievement which Kev still manages to maintain to this day, leading to his occasional labelling in posts by others on the Vapors Fan Group page as "Mr Too Cool For Facebook"). The Vapors straw broke my own particular camel's back, however, and primarily in order to keep abreast of the unfolding band news, I finally signed up and succumbed to a life of likes, shares, tags and becoming "friends" with, well, some friends, and many more people who I may have bumped into once or twice.

Things became clearer, and a series of gigs was announced for October and November, opening not in Guildford or London, but in Dublin, to be followed by the first London show since Roehampton, at a venue whose very name (albeit marginally altered location) sent sentimental shivers that emanated straight from those late 70's NME gig guides down the spine, Dingwall's in Camden Lock. There would be two further gigs, in Wolverhampton and Liverpool, and tickets were made available. We made our plans, and got in touch with Shaun Modern, who had taken on management duties for the band's reincarnation and who agreed to arrange after show party entry for us following the Dublin gig. We began counting the days, weeks and months. Kev rung me at one point, and rather oddly asked me what size T-shirt I wore, which I thought at the time was a somewhat bizarre question as we had already pre-ordered our new for 2016 Vapors tour T-shirts for collection in Dublin, but I answered the question and thought no more of it.

Earlier that year, after a false start and never really off the ground reunion discussion early on in the century, a chain of events had fallen into place. Dave Fenton had retired, and, perhaps still harbouring one last desire to produce that third album, messaged Steve, Howard and Ed saying nothing more than "I've got a proposition I want to make, fancy a drink?"

Ed rang Steve, basically to ask what he thought of the message, and they agreed that they certainly had nothing to lose by meeting up for a beer. Steve freely admits to sitting on the train on his way up for the meeting, not having seen Dave for several years, wondering in depth what would unfold, what he'd say, but in his words "The evening was perfect and we all began to think, right what can we do together?"

Dave's little known first public airing of "Turning Japanese" in over 30 years had come a few years previously at Dan's sixth form end of school year bash, snappily named the "Senior Prefect's Week of Fun." "The school arranged a number of events and Friday's was a combination of music and dance that had to be organised by the senior prefects" explains Dan. "We were split into four houses at school and the theme for the night was 'Decades' with each house having to put something on for their nominated era. We were given the 80s!"

The deputy head was a big music fan, as it seems were several of the teachers, many of whom were of a certain age and knew of Dan's family background, periodically nagging him to see what he could cajole his father into doing at the school. "So here I am, having to organise some 80s music for the school show, with the deputy head prodding me and just saying 'Go on, ask your dad!'" By all accounts it took some persuading, but on that Friday night, a "mystery guest" took to the stage, accompanied by Dan and the band that he had already put together, and who were already playing regularly, and sang "Turning Japanese." Dan laughs at the recollection. "The teachers went madder than anyone! They were like 'What?!' and he sang the song standing up with no guitar to hide behind, not knowing what to do with his hands! Halfway through the bassist trod on his lead and broke the plug, so a guy got up on stage and held it in the amp for the rest of the song. Dad said at the end 'Oh, looks like we've got a new roadie.' It was the headmaster!"

It would appear that no recordings have surfaced of the evening, which is perhaps for the best, but it was soon to be repeated. "Next time he sang it was at my 18th. We had a little covers band come in and mum said, 'Don't suppose you know Turning Japanese?' And they said, 'Yeah, it's on our setlist actually!' and mum just shrugged in dad's direction and said, 'Well he wrote it!' So he sang it with them too. Maybe that got the ball rolling, maybe that's when he finally thought 'Oh you know what, I can do it.'"

In the spring of 2016, The Shakespearos were playing Polyfest, an annual all-day charity event held in the memory of punk legend Poly Styrene, at The Half Moon in Putney. "Turning Japanese" had always been a part of their repertoire, and Steve remembers the organiser, by all accounts one of the London music scene's great eccentrics, repeatedly pestering him to get The Vapors involved. Following their meeting, and with Ed and Dave both available, Steve invited the pair of them along to the evening gig, and when it came to the performance of "Turning

Japanese", Dave and Ed clambered on stage with Steve for the first time since 1981.

Du Kane performed rhythm guitar duties, leaving Dave once again guitar-free and not quite sure what to do with his hands, so there followed a brief routine of gentle middle-aged pogoing and Japanese martial arts moves as he approached the microphone, the likes of which have never been seen in public again since, whilst the crowd cheered in anticipation. He grabbed the microphone and the band launched into one of the lesser polished deliveries of the song that has spanned the decades, but that wasn't really the point.

"The Internet just went mad" says Steve "and the clamour was incredible. Shaun Modern, who we didn't know then, got in touch out of the blue and offered to help out, he knew the other Shaun who promoted the first few gigs, and those first four shows were booked. Shaun Modern was a legend, there was nothing he couldn't do to help, and the rest is history!"

Howard, having just consciously walked away from his record shop to commit to his young family, stuck to that decision, but has kept a close and friendly eye as events have unfolded since, occasionally contributing on the fans page on Facebook. Turning their attention to finding an appropriate drummer, Dave suggested to Steve and Ed that he had someone in mind, but they'd have to see what they thought. "I got the call from Dave after he'd done that Half Moon thing" Michael explains. "I had kept occasionally in touch with Dave and Branka, I'd been to see the kids when they were young, so it wasn't completely out of the blue, but it was Dave's idea and I'd need to audition for Ed and Steve before we thought any more about it." He played for Steve, who liked what he saw, and then Ed, who felt the same, and from that point on the band were once again a working four-piece and they began to practise individually and rehearse together, often with Dan filling in for Ed on guitar so that the other three of them could continue to work as a unit even whilst Ed was away filming.

And so, the time came. Thirty-five and a half years after that gig at Roehampton and I was off to see The Vapors. Last time round we'd bunked the bus to the gig, blagged our way into the soundcheck so that we could sponge a place on the guest list and walked back through the night to Victoria Station, and all it had cost us was the effort spent by Kev's mum baking.

This time there was a weekend away in a vibrant European city, air travel and a swanky boutique hotel involved. 35 years without The Vapors had given me the opportunity to get married, build a decent career, live comfortably, raise a family and continue my music obsession with attendance at any number of gigs. Many of which were truly average, and many of which were truly memorable. But none of them were quite *the same*. None of them came with the increased heart rate, sense of expectation, or general excitement of going to see *our band*.

Colin was unable to make the Dublin gig, but Kev and I arranged to meet up there and make a weekend of it, and so on Thursday 13th October 2016 I found myself at Gatwick Airport, gig ticket and minimal changes of clothing packed into hand luggage, waiting to fly to Dublin. I'd made the short drive to the airport accompanied by the sound of The Vapors compilation CD with the volume cranked up to full and sat in the car for 20 minutes once I'd parked just to let the CD reach its conclusion. Travelling to the terminal I was as excited as I'd ever been before checking in to any flight to go anywhere for any reason. Arriving at Dublin Airport and getting a taxi into the city centre (another travel mode first for a Vapors gig) I bemused the Albanian driver with my story about why I was there, what I was going to do, and just how brilliant the whole thing was. As usual of course there was a gleam of recognition when I trotted out the "You've probably never heard of them, but you'd recognise their big hit single" line, but by and large I sensed that he was confused by the fact that he'd just picked up a hyper-active teenager trapped in a 52 year old man's slightly past-its-prime body.

Kev flew out from Frankfurt, and made more of a connection with his taxi driver, a native Irishman who knew not only of the band, but of the venue, and every other venue in Dublin, and who claimed to have driven every cool rock star who had ever visited Dublin around (and some who probably hadn't) and been to so many gigs over the last 40 years that sheer mathematics would probably prove impossible.

We met at the hotel, sipped some cappuccinos and checked into our rooms, before heading out for a night in the bars of Dublin catching up, discussing politics and the real world, drinking Guinness and of course anticipating the promise of the following night.

Kev had ordered his ticket online for collection and despite having spent years as a world-renowned, successful international car designer, well-versed in foreign travel, deadlines, and just plain getting things done, he was not going to relax until he had his guaranteed entry for the following evening confirmed. He was determined that he was going to locate and clasp his hands around his golden ticket from the venue at the first available opportunity, so before he would allow us into a bar, he insisted that we head off to find the Opium Room on Wexford Street.

We followed our Google Maps inspired instincts and located the venue, which turned out to be one block from the hotel on an already busy early-evening, bar-strewn bustle of a thoroughfare, and learned from someone out front that the entrance to The Opium Room auditorium that formed a part of the labyrinthine structure of the Whelan's venue could be located around the back, in Liberty Lane. We wandered around the corner into a typically tatty litter-strewn and windswept city backstreet and I propped myself against a makeshift temporary support comprised of wheelie bins and a lamppost whilst Kev tried a few doors. I had tried to persuade Kev that if he'd ordered his ticket from Ticketmaster, then there would be no issue with picking it up the following evening when the venue actually opened, but he wasn't to be thwarted. I slumped disinterestedly further back onto my somewhat uncomfortable and ever so slightly smelly resting place, muttering something about the pubs being open and us being in Dublin, as Kev managed to find a door that actually opened, and disappeared through it in some form of bizarre, inner-city, urban Narnia fashion.

Thirty minutes of heel kicking later, Kev re-emerged, ticketless but somewhat animated. He had met a member of the venue's staff as he entered the place, who had informed him that Ticketmaster had an outlet in the City Centre where he would be able to collect his ticket, but on listening to Kev's hyped-up childlike excited explanation of why he was there, offered to show him around the venue. Kev emerged with misty eyes and a tale to tell. "It's perfect!" he blurted in a high-pitched state of glee. "It's small, there's a big long bar, it's dark and smelly, the floor's all sticky, and the guy even showed me the toilets." Delighted of course to learn this, I asked politely if we could now go to the pub but was told that no, we needed to head towards St Stephens Green Shopping Centre, where the Ticketmaster kiosk would still be open.

Sensing he was not going to back down, or indeed relax, until we had done so, I wearily agreed. We arrived at the booth, to be told, somewhat unsurprisingly, that if he had ordered the ticket for venue collection, he would be able to collect the ticket at the venue.

With Kev finally convinced, we headed to the pub and pulled up two bar stools. There were now two teenagers trapped in 52 year old bodies, and we covered all sorts of important ground, such as what songs they might play the following night, what they might look like, what would the new drummer bring to the band, how would they handle the recorded "bwoo, woo, woo" bits in "Turning Japanese" that we both vaguely remembered them having difficulty with live back in 1980 and 1981. Who would be there? Would there be any fans from the old days that we remembered and had lost touch with? Would there be other fans from back in the day with stories to tell? What would the band members actually be like? Would they be the same friendly, down to earth guys we remembered from back then, or was that just rose-tinted spectacles? And above all, of course, would they actually be any good?

"I tell you what we definitely won't hear," said Kev, "Sunstroke, y'know, the B-side of 'Prisoners', they'll never play that!"

"Yeah," I agreed. "I'm sure we'll hear 'Magnets' though," I laughed, "it'll give them the excuse to do that 'we're going to slow things down now with a couple of acoustic numbers' thing mid-set."

Kev asked me mysteriously to make sure that I remembered to remind him the following day that he had something he had to take to the gig but wouldn't tell me what.

We chatted the night away, rose in the morning and enjoyed a sensible pre-gig Irish breakfast that we agreed both of our mothers would have heartily approved of given our plans for the next sixteen hours or so, before heading into the city for some brief sightseeing and less brief celebration of the Temple Bar, Dublin, interpretation of Irish culture.

Still relatively sober, we headed back to the hotel, freshened up, and headed out to a bar around the corner from the venue, with Kev clutching his mysterious package to his side. We got talking to a couple of guys in the bar, boring more locals with the whole story about why we were there, but by now our emotions were running high.

"Are you two OK?" one of them asked in that quizzical, friendly Dublin accent that endears itself easily to people the world over.

"Yes of course, why wouldn't we be?" we replied in unison.

"It's just that you're both a ghostly shade of white, and you're shaking?" contributed his friend, phrasing the observation as a question.

We realised simultaneously that here we both were, an hour before the doors opened for the most important gig that either of us had been to since 1981, not to put too fine a point on it, crapping ourselves. What if nobody actually turned up? What if the band were shit? What if the next few hours of our lives destroyed a legacy that we both cherished so highly? Neither of us had appeared to consider these possibilities during the excitement of the announcement of the reformation, the scheduling of the gigs, or the build up to the trip to Dublin, but now we were on the verge of witnessing history, and suddenly both realising that there had to be a chance that it could all go horribly wrong.

Dave Fenton admits to being nervous before every performance he has ever given, so compared to our anxiety goodness only knows what he was going through, but at least he had the knowledge that the band had prepared, rehearsed and treated the whole adventure in a hugely professional manner, something which we wouldn't see the evidence of for ourselves until later that evening.

We needn't have worried, of course. As soon as we entered the venue (after Kev had of course collected his ticket at the door with zero complications) we heard a bunch of familiar, high quality tunes from our golden era, expertly spun by RTE presenter, DJ and partner of Shaun Modern, our friend-to-be, Jacqui Carroll. We found and introduced ourselves to modern day hero Shaun Modern, whose efforts had been so instrumental in putting the whole thing together. We made our way to the merchandise stand to pick up our pre-ordered T-shirts, we met some other fans who had flown, literally, from all over the world, and at some point that evening the 21st century version of The Vapors Family came into existence.

Way before the band came on, the nerves had gone. The place just *felt* right. The openness and friendliness we experienced from people who would soon become valued friends, the atmosphere generated by the music being played, and the sense of palpable anticipation amongst what was not a sell-out audience, but not an insignificant one either, combined with the Guinness to provide an exhilarating sense of well-being.

Local band The Dubtones opened up and played a blistering 30-minute set that just enhanced the mood, and before we knew it the time was coming.

No standing-by-the-mixing-desk nonsense for us that night. We headed to the front of the auditorium and took our place alongside a number of other people who we also didn't know at the time would soon become firm friends, and amongst whom excited conversations took place about where the last time everyone was when they saw the band, where they'd come from, how they were related to the band and, most of all, how excited everyone was. There was no cynicism, no doubt, no nervousness anymore. There was just an all-encompassing feeling of camaraderie that, in a nutshell, defines the social circle that envelops this band, their families, their management and crew, and their fans, and gets stronger every time we all come together.

Set lists were taped down. Kev couldn't resist a peek. I told him I just didn't want to know, that I wanted to be surprised. So he had a look and glanced back at me with a sense of slightly nonplussed amusement that was the best way he could find of not spoiling it for me.

The lights went down, the band's entrance soundtrack was played, and there they were. Unmistakably, David, Steven and Edward, all familiar in their looks and their mannerisms, all looking about 35 years older than they had looked 35 years ago, all looking content and like they had lived good lives, but not so good that they had aged in anything other than a natural way.

And then there was Michael, the new drummer. He walked on stage, about eight feet tall, he sat down and he begun bashing the living daylight out of his drums with a massive, genuine, fixed smile on his face that has been omnipresent in every performance since.

The band launched straight into their traditional set-opener of old and live favourite (but never released) "Secret Noise" and if any of us did have any concerns about quality control left at that point they were banished within seconds. The band could play. With hindsight of course they always had been able to, but the mists of time had perhaps contributed to their polished musicianship being one of the lesser memories of the whole first-time-round live Vapors experience.

Ed's big 80s hair has long since disappeared, but his rock guitar shapes, riffs and solos contributed to the songs as much as they had ever done. Steve's hair was, and remains, intact as does his extraordinary "lead" bass guitar ability, also being a defining sound of the band. And Dave's rhythm guitar, but more importantly his voice, remain capable of delivering the classic songs he penned all those years ago. Michael's drumming brought a new dynamic to the performance. It's difficult to compare a set performed by a bunch of sixty-something year-olds to the same set performed at the height of the New Wave boom, but the technical ability, the energy and the professionalism of old were very much there to see. With the addition of a drummer who genuinely looks like he's playing every song as if his life depended on it but is celebrating that life at the same time. Howard's drumming in the original line-up was outstanding, and it is unfair and pointless to compare the two, but the fact that the band had replaced Howard with someone who brings something different to the band rather than just hiring an identikit session drummer is all part of the modern-day magic. The lack of one of the original members of the band had the potential to diminish the story, but the reality is that the opposite happened, and the recruitment of Michael enhanced it.

The band moved on to what is still my personal favourite of all of their singles, "News At Ten", and ripped through the majority of debut album "New Clear Days" and selected songs from "Magnets" with a couple of classic B-sides thrown in for good measure. Rather inevitably, "Magnets" itself was not played, but "Sunstroke" was. So much for myself and Kev's fan expertise in song selection.

If the band themselves had been nervous (and they were, Branka recalling that "we needed two buckets in the dressing room that night, one for Dave and one for Ed!") it didn't show. They quickly relaxed, aided no doubt by the fact that they had an audience that were very firmly onside, and the between song banter was relaxed, celebratory and self-deprecating in exactly the right measures. In cliched fashion it was over too soon, and the band were encoring with traditional set closer "Here Comes The Judge".

The band left the stage, the lights went up and Jacqui continued to play the perfect occasion-relevant mix of tunes. I remember looking very deliberately around myself before we all began to drift away from the stage, and the memory of a bunch of never-to-be-strangers-again folk just smiling at each other for what seemed like an eternity will last with me for ever.

And so, proudly brandishing our wristbands, we made our way around the corner, through another auditorium in the same catacomb of a venue, and upstairs to the designated after-show party area.

Some of the people we had been smiling with a few minutes previously were there, as were some other people who we got chatting to who were variously band-members' family, old friends or old fans. Before long, the band walked in to a rousing and impromptu cheer, looking relieved, proud and relaxed.

It is, of course, the music, the sound, the legacy of a strong set of recorded material, and the quality of the live performance, that will draw people back time and again to the same band. But the next few hours reminded us why this band had held such a special place in our memories. Immediately they entered the room they spread out amongst us and began chatting away like old friends about the first-time round, the intervening 35 years, why they'd got back together, how their family lives had developed, and just about any other subject that was raised. But most of all, the genuine, heartfelt thanks that was offered to us all that night, just for turning up, was neither patronising nor manufactured. There's a bit of rock'n'roll to every band member's personality, but conceited stars they most definitely are not. The affirmation that our recollections were accurate, that these were genuine nice guys, that our judgement as teenagers had been right, and that the emotional memories were not only valid but being built upon, spawned the positivity that has carried The Vapors Family throughout the subsequent three years.

As we chatted to Ed, Kev finally moved towards his hitherto untouched package. "You probably won't remember this," he grinned, "but at some point in 1980, you called me at home one night to say that you had a spare 'News At Ten' T-shirt." Ed immediately apologised for indeed not remembering, somewhat missing the point. Kev laughed, before continuing "I never repaid the debt though, so I've had these made" pulling out a set of pristine 2016 remakes of the original 1980s "News At Ten" promotional shirts and presenting one to Ed.

Again, Ed's overwhelmed thanks and gratitude rings clear in the mind, and despite the fact that this was Kev's way of trying to say thanks for the friendship and unflinching, accommodating assistance that these guys had given us all those years ago, here was one of them again giving us the gratitude.

Further shirts were presented to Dave, Steve and Michael, all also received with equal appreciation, the latter of whose introduction to the Vapors fan group that night was clearly being enjoyed by himself as much as the performance had been, and who was fascinated by the 36-years-ago T-shirt tale. Finally understanding Kev's question of several months previously, he presented me with one too, and had one ready for Colin next time we saw him.

We met various other family members and various other fans all, as hoped, with tales to tell from the old days, and spent most of the rest of the night sat down drinking beer with Steve, somehow trying to catch up on thirty-plus years of life and chucking in the occasional memory of gigs from the past. I learnt that Steve was now living in Sussex, just a few miles from me in Brighton, and we discussed everything from music, football, travel, growing old and respectable (in some measure) to our respective kids' upbringing and schooling in the area local to us. We made provisional arrangements to meet up locally for a beer or two, something which has become a most enjoyable, regular by-product of The Vapors reforming.

Steve, Kev, myself and the others sat at our table were the last to leave the venue, and as we did so we were very aware of the special evening we had experienced, tired but relieved, contented and excited for the future in equal measures.

We already had tickets for the Dingwall's show, a couple of weeks later, but Steve gave us the nod about an unannounced free warm-up gig in Guildford that the band were planning for the next weekend. Although not a music venue back in the 70s and 80s, The Holroyd Arms, situated a few hundred yards from one of the band's old stomping grounds, The Wooden Bridge, is now one of the town's regular music venues. Run by an old mate of Steve's, it was an obvious choice for a low-key preparation exercise prior to the high-profile London show the following week.

For the second time in my life, and the second time in a week, I checked into a hotel room close to the venue of a Vapors gig, and headed straight to the pub. As I walked into the front bar, a very typical and slightly old-school edge-of-town establishment complete with regulation dartboards and technicolour star shaped stickers advertising chips and other staple foods falling under the "Traditional British pub meal" banner, the band were just starting their soundcheck.

There were a handful of obviously pub locals drinking in the bar, and a handful of obviously Vapors fans who had arrived early in the pub's tiny back music room, some of whom were familiar from the previous week's adventure. We greeted each other like long lost friends as the band ran through some songs, including something that, like the entire experience of actually seeing them play live, none of us had considered very likely up till a few weeks previously, a new song. "Sundown River" has always been one of the stronger of the many new songs the band now have in their repertoire, and has been polished and refined in the three years since, but even then in an empty back room of a small pub on a Sunday teatime, hearing Dave's vocals effectively rehearsing something new, and listening to the song's musical twists, was a spine-tingling moment. At first hearing, it immediately evoked some deep, dormant feelings, unmistakably The Vapors, but sounding simultaneously fresh and new, influenced lyrically and structurally by 35 years of Dave's life and 35 years of the development of rock music.

The band came over and said hello, once again brimming with thanks and slightly bemused humility that people had made the effort, oblivious to the fact that it felt that we should be the ones thanking them. Ed introduced me to a handful of other early arrivals, who in turn introduced me to friends of their own as they arrived, one of whom, to my amazement and unbridled delight was wearing a Piranhas badge, taking me even further back than The Vapors could do, and we spent most of the evening socialising in the most celebratory yet relaxed way imaginable. A number of the people I met that night would of course have been in that Marquee audience back in 1980, and several are still active in the local music scene in Guildford. For all the talk (a lot based on grim reality of course) of the loss of live venues, and the corresponding risk to music in all of its diverse forms, it is heart-warming to follow the exploits of these people on Facebook as they contribute to what is quite clearly still a vibrant Guildford music scene.

The band played a full set to a relatively small crowd as Dave observed sardonically that "It was supposed to be a secret gig, but this is maybe a bit too secret" but that was of no concern to any of us there in what felt like, however low-key, a triumphant homecoming. The band started slowly, but four or five songs in Michael seemed to glance around himself in a very calculated and deliberate way, before beginning to bash the living daylights out of his drums with an extra vigour, and the band responded. As has become the norm, the band asked us afterwards how it had sounded, and the concerned attention they pay to the answers they get is a testament to how seriously they are taking the whole thing. I've mentioned to them on many occasions that they could probably forget all the words and each play four different songs at the same time, and we wouldn't really care, but in reality the attention they pay to quality control during each and every gig is impressive, even if sometimes the sense of occasion feels like that is of greater importance to us fans.

With it being a relaxed Sunday evening, and being in a local pub rather than a commercially run venue, there was no pressure to leave, and gradually the band and those audience members who had remained for a drink drifted out to the pub's outdoor seating area. Talk was fairly obviously about the band, but with the slightly different demographic to the previous week, conversations began to drift towards more general 70s and 80s reminiscences, fairly obviously The Jam and The Stranglers given the locality, but also with a general "So what have you been doing for the last 35 years?" thread that would normally be reserved for old acquaintances, the only difference being that a lot of those there, although undoubtedly having been at the same place at the same time, were meeting for the first time, or at least knowingly doing so.

After seemingly chatting with everyone there, I sat down at a pub bench next to a dark-haired, Vapors T-shirt-clad woman puffing away on a vape. "Hello, I'm Dave's wife", she announced matter-of-factly with a smile, and I introduced myself to Branka.

For some reason I decided it was necessary to recount every moment I could recall of my memories of Dave, which as I began to run through them, I became very conscious of being very few and far between compared to those I had of Ed and Steve. I'm not sure why that seemed so important or why I thought she'd care given that clearly, she had spent half her life with him, and as I have got to know her since have learned first-hand that she's not shy when it comes to having a story to tell herself. But she listened politely, chatted in a way that was nothing but friendly and interested, and we looked forward as excitedly as one another to the following week's gig, which was beginning to feel like it was going to be something of a very special occasion.

One Of My Dreams

Although only up the road in London, with the Dingwall's gig being on a Friday, there was no question of risking a last minute dash from work, so I booked the day off and arranged to meet Colin and Kev, who in turn had arranged to meet Pete, who had last seen The Vapors in Brighton in 1981, and who I hadn't seen since the day we left school.

Not wanting to risk having to hang about at railway stations, anxiously or otherwise, for any reason, I headed into Brighton for what would I am sure have been another fully endorsed mother-approved level of pre-alcohol intake cooked breakfast and made my way straight to the station to head up to London giving myself half a day to spare.

We made plans to meet in a Camden pub in the early afternoon and shared the location on the fans' group Facebook page, primarily as I had promised some of the people I had met in Guildford the previous week that I would, but also as an open invitation. By late afternoon, the first incarnation of what is now a customary and treasured Vapors Family tradition, the mass pre-gig meet-up, was well underway.

I hadn't seen Pete for 35 years, but although we had spoken regularly in the lead-up it was the first time I had seen Colin for many years as well. Pete brought a son along, I managed to persuade Beccy to come and see what all the fuss was about, and our number were joined by members of the Guildford fraternity we'd met the previous week and others from the Facebook page who had also planned to make a day of it. Once again the conversation veered from misty-eyed memories, to catching up on 35 years of news, to excitement about the band, to contemporary music, to football, to the level of pleasure and excitement the new Vapors experience was beginning to engender, or would begin to engender for the first time that evening, and round and round again.

Dingwall's is another London venue with an evocative name, steeped in history and tradition, right up there with The Marquee in my mind in the golden memory list of early 80s gig attendance. It had been many years since I last went there, probably not since the 80s themselves in fact. Steve had warned me at Guildford to expect it to be slightly different to how I remembered it, which I took as a negative, but what he had neglected to mention, and that I was completely unaware of, was that it had metamorphosed into a completely different building.

On arrival, however, I was soon put at ease. The new venue maintained all necessary 80s Dingwallian features. The iconic brickwork of the Victorian canal-side Camden Lock buildings had been spruced up but was intact and the interior of the club still had all requisite component ingredients. A long bar at the back gave way to a standing platform, in turn leading to two or three steps down to an archetypal London music venue dance floor in front of a cramped but fit for purpose stage. The venue, sold out for the band's first London gig since the Roehampton daffodil and power failure spectacular, was already full, even before the arrival of the night's support act. The (then) current line-up of Department S, whose original incarnation's arrival on the music scene, and the occasion of their best-known single "Is Vic There?" had overlapped with the end of the original Vapors' existence, played a well-received set to the already full house, and drinks were recharged for the main event.

Following the fun in Dublin, and still in early teenage front of stage mode rather than later teenage sound-desk audience mode, we made our way to a point directly in front of Ed's microphone and joined a number of rapidly becoming familiar faces. We were astonished to meet some friends from Brighton who were stood in exactly the same place, together with their grown-up daughter who Beccy had last seen when she was babysitting for her aged about five. Never mind Dave's apologetic on-stage explanations for singing songs in his sixties that referenced sixteen-year-old girls, this certainly placed some context around the generational shift that had occurred since the last time these songs were performed in London for us.

Beccy's previously quipped comment voicing her concerns about the space restricting potential of fans of a certain age proved prophetic, as the minds attached to the fifty-something year old beer guts reverted immediately to the 70s whilst the guts themselves remained firmly rooted in the present, simultaneously wobbling out of control as they moshed, pogoed and leapt to the first few Vapors numbers. The Dublin crowd had been loud and enthusiastic, this one was the same in double measure with added boisterousness thrown in until stamina lapsed about fifteen minutes in. It was amiable and fun though, never unpleasant, with the stamped upon toes, accidental pushes and off-balance shoves all being accompanied with perfectly delivered apologies. Polite punk for the post-parenthood generation was a joy to be enmeshed in.

Aside from the crowd excitement, The Vapors played a stormer. The atmosphere was right, the sell-out crowd's enthusiasm undoubtedly fuelled the band, and their subsequent game-raising in turn fired the crowd some more. Dublin had been a true, professional performance, but not unexpectedly it bore all the hallmarks of a band performing in public for the first time in over three decades. The Guildford warm-up had started slowly and gathered steam, but all things considered, that was exactly what it was, a warm-up. This was different altogether. It's easy to forget sometimes amongst the excitement of live rock and roll, but what makes a good band, funnily enough, is that they deliver music in an accomplished and talented way. Inject some energy and a receptive audience and the event can quickly become a temporary but euphoric celebration of release from the cares of the world, and the following ninety minutes of sweat inside a canal-side building in Camden Town were exactly that.

Beccy and I made our way home, the others stayed behind for what became, by the sounds of it, a rather long and celebratory after show party. The band had already announced a follow-up show in London scheduled for the following spring, completing the perfect hat-trick of legendary venues from my youth by being booked for Oxford Street's 100 Club. Buoyed by sales for those first few reformation gigs, tickets had been made available in advance to fans that night at Dingwall's, so with another two safely stowed in my pocket we made our way home happy with the memories, their still recent rebirth, and the promise of more to come.

There were two other gigs on that brief tour, in Wolverhampton and Liverpool, and although I flirted with the idea of travelling up to them I was still just about in grown up adult fan mode at that point, the full time return to teenage obligatory attendance at every opportunity rule only being invoked during an interrupted by ill-health 2017 and applied in full in 2018.

Spring came around soon enough, and another Holroyd Arms warm up gig was arranged for the week before the 100 Club show. Whether word had spread locally better this time round, or whether Steve's April Fool's day double bluff of placing a notice on Facebook announcing that "Guildford's best Vapors tribute band, Secret Noise" would be playing at the pub that evening had the desired effect, the pub filled up early on this occasion. I've yet to come across a Vapors tribute act, but there's still time.

The increasingly familiar usual local and not so local suspects turned up, another new song was aired, and the atmosphere was somewhere between a low-key and low-pressure warm-up, a private party and a growing, collective, joyous realisation that it was looking like the previous autumn's outing might not just have been a commemorative reunion, but the start of a new adventure. The standard was good, and the post-gig pub garden assembly lasted late and fostered less of the usual retro chat, and a lot more looking forward.

The 100 Club pre-show get together was scheduled, at Ed's recommendation, in Bradley's Spanish Bar, tucked in a tiny cut-through between Oxford Street and Tottenham

Court Road, with many more fans turning up, mostly now proudly sporting 21st century Vapors T-shirts, than the bar could accommodate. Fortunately, it was the sort of sunny spring day that for me makes Central London as enjoyable a place to relax as pretty much any other location in the country. We spilled out into the street, annoying a succession of passing cabbies who delighted in informing us that we were blocking a public highway. To our growing amusement, with the alcohol intake undoubtedly contributing to an increasing sense of hilarity, various Vapors fans began taking up deliberately convoluted positions in the quiet side street in an attempt to create some form of giant Taxi slalom course and further irritate their drivers.

Fans arrived from all over the country, and again from all over the world, and we were joined by Branka and Dan who assured us the band had been safely installed inside the legendary venue. Another strong bill had been arranged, with support coming from yet another band steeped in punk era folklore, The Members, and once again the venue was full early on. Like Dingwall's, it had been a long time since I'd seen the inside of the 100 Club, but unlike Dingwall's, the interior was identical to its early 80s self. The stairs down from the streets are still adorned with posters, portraits and photographs of some of the legends that have performed there since the second world war, including the Jazz greats for which it was originally known, and the increasing number of now household rock acts that have graced its stage since it adopted its current name in the year I was born. As the stairs opened out into the long, rectangular auditorium, stage set unusually along one of the long sides of the rectangle, I glanced left and right at the bars at each of its shorter ends, noting that everything was exactly where I remembered it, instantly being transported back to somewhere in nineteen eighty something.

"Not sure why The Members are supporting us, think we should be supporting them" Steve had grinned at me in typical self-effacing style the week before. I don't think the majority of the evening's audience that night would have agreed with him, but they produced a polished, expertly accelerating set which of course culminated in "Sound Of The Suburbs" and of course was very warmly received.

I spent the entirety of The Vapors set locked at the front of the stage with an ever-increasing number of pogoing beer guts (for the record, Kev and Colin being notable exceptions to this body shaming generalisation). Unlike Dingwall's, and I am sure in no way connected to the extended hospitality of Bradley's Spanish Bar that afternoon, I flipped into "If you can't beat them join them" mode and spent the entire show leaping around in a physically foolish, and I am sure visually foolish, 90 minutes of age denial.

Beccy had retreated to the safety of the side of the stage and watched the gig in altogether more sensible style with various members of the band's families, whilst I somehow got through the whole set without hitting the ground, apart from when I was picking myself up from it. It was probably the first time since 1984, probably at Dingwall's and probably in the company of Norwich's finest, Serious Drinking, a band I saw often and whose performances demanded an obvious adherence to their name, that I had behaved like that throughout a gig. And it was certainly the last.

Despite our somewhat different gig experiences that night, Beccy and I agreed the show had been exceptional yet again. With the band scheduled for a number of gigs up and down the country for the rest of the year, along with the arrival of new songs and the promise of more, things were really on the rise. This now had the feel that it was becoming something more than a happy trip down memory lane.

I began snapping up tickets, deciding against going to another return to Camden gig at The Roundhouse in June, where this time it was the band's turn to support another legendary punk outfit, The Skids, which is a decision I regret, although by all accounts it wasn't The Vapors' finest hour as they were beset by sound problems. The Skids, however, were apparently everything that they were remembered for and more, and certainly the quality of their own new material would suggest that would probably have been the case. With the last intact vestiges of my Vapors-related adult common sense I also decided against a trip to Scotland for a couple of gigs arranged there for later in June, and also against the trek to their Blackpool appearance at the annual Rebellion punk festival and a similar one at Butlins in Skegness.

Tickets were, however, booked for gigs in Norwich, Shoreham-By-Sea (as close to a hometown Vapors gig as I'd ever been able to attend), Bristol, Salisbury (where they were to be reunited with Bruce Foxton, supporting his From The Jam outfit) and London again, at the 229 venue in Great Portland Street. A ticket and hotel booking were also secured for the final gig of the year, a Christmas special booked at Portmeirion, a notable location for so many reasons, not least of which that it was used to film 60s TV classic "The

Prisoner", which had been the inspiration for The Vapors' 1979 debut single. Booking the village's hall for the Christmas knees-up was therefore an inspired choice, and the band elected to use the occasion to undertake that most modern of rock traditions, play the first album in its entirety from start to finish.

Tickets safely acquired, the gigs began to roll around. Prior to the 100 Club show I had engaged in a long online chat one evening using my newly found social media expertise with a guy called Owen Carne. Owen had missed out on The Vapors first time round, but their recorded material had always been high on his favourites list, so when the reunification came around his gig attendance compulsiveness was equal to, or truth be told, greater than my own. We'd met at several of those early reunion gigs, however on one evening early in 2017 we engaged in a long chat centred around the band that had first stoked my fire, The Stranglers. Although slightly younger than me and having not been able to see his own first musical love until later than I was lucky enough to have done, it quickly became apparent that any obsessional gig related behaviour I demonstrated was merely a drop in the ocean set against Owen's and that of his wife Jacquie. Veterans of well over 400 Stranglers gigs, each one diligently recorded in an Excel spreadsheet, they are well known amongst that particular band's still not inconsiderable fan base, with Owen running the band's website and regularly organising coach trips to groups of European gigs as they continue regular touring.

I made the mistake of mentioning to Owen that I had kind of fallen out of love with The Stranglers quite early in the 1980s, and well before Hugh Cornwell had left, and that I couldn't really see the point of them anymore. With reasoned online skills of diplomacy and encouragement he persuaded me to be a little more open minded, and we met at the band's Brighton gig in March of that year, a couple of weeks before The Vapors returned to live action. He was right. Jean-Jacques and Dave still produce the band's unique sound, new member (well, 19 year stalwart as guitarist and 15 years as singer actually) Baz Warne complements but doesn't just ape the original holder of those roles, and a replacement for the sadly necessarily retired through age and health Jet Black on drums does nothing to dampen the band dynamic. I still never really look beyond the band's first four albums for home Stranglers entertainment, but returning regularly to their live shows of late after so long has been a bonus and enjoyable surprise.

So, by the time of the Norwich gig in June, Owen and myself had become regular Vapors partners in crime and I now count him as one of my very good friends. We met up in a riverside pub close to the venue, with a smaller group of regulars present than usual, presumably due to the city's relatively remote location from some of the country's more populous areas. Nevertheless, we were joined by an ever more familiar bunch of faces, including Graham and Karen who had made the not insignificant trip from Cornwall, just about as far from Norwich as you can get in England, Elaine Bevan and Jane Wadman who were fast becoming stalwarts themselves, and a number of others. The gig was another triumph, in stark contrast I learned, to the previous evening's Skids support slot, and all returned to hotels happy, band and fans alike.

The following weekend saw two of the shows that I had decided not to travel to, in Scotland, and that for the first time provided a logistical clash for Ed, who was away filming with commitments that he couldn't alter. Dave's son Dan had known the songs for years, of course, and had helped the reformed band with rehearsals in Ed's absence, but this would be the first time he'd have to be called off the sub's bench to play them at live shows. "It wasn't really mentioned as a possibility the year before" he recalls. "But the Rebellion booking had already needed to be confirmed earlier in the year, and although that gig wasn't until August, Ed knew he wouldn't be able to make it, so we'd already all kind of agreed that I'd help out when required, and we'll see how it goes." The evidence seems to suggest that it went just fine. The reality is that Dan, despite his lack of formal training, is an exceptionally talented guitarist. In the same way as Michael's replacement of Howard for the reformation a year previously had freshened the sound, rather than necessarily improving or diminishing it, Dan's playing is different to Ed's, but I don't think I've ever felt since that I'd prefer it if one or other of them were playing.

My thoughts turned to Shoreham, a few weeks later, and a show I was particularly looking forward to due to its proximity to Brighton. I had already informed Kev and Colin that attendance was compulsory, and we set about making a weekend of it.

My youngest sister, who had had to endure my record collection thumping through the flimsy post-war constructed bedroom walls of our house during the majority of her own formative years, but who has professed to at least a respect for The Vapors' music ever since, came along with her partner, a chilled out, reggae loving music fan with wide eclectic tastes of a different sort who I suspected beforehand may not quite enjoy the whole event to quite the same extent.

Pre-gig warm-up duly sorted for the pub opposite the venue, we once again started early and a good crowd turned up, swelled by a number of the Guildford contingent who had made the short trip down to the coast. The evening was notable for the first public appearance that I had been aware of at a pre-gig meeting of a legendary piece of documentation, the Vapors Family's very own Domesday artefact, Elaine Bevan's scrapbook.

A number of the now regular group of fans, Elaine and Rob Payne amongst them, but also including a number of the still based in Guildford original set of Vapors fans and friends that would turn up at most of the South East shows had, by the time of the Shoreham gig, already discussed on numerous occasions all of the events we recalled from the early days. Connections were made between us that we never knew existed, but which evidently had to have been there all along. Amongst the Guildford crowd's own group of friends was Tim Cox, a guy who has spent his whole life in the music business, pretty much starting out as The Vapors' most trusted roadie and guitar technician in 1979, and who has worked across the world supporting the on-stage musical element of countless other bands' touring requirements ever since. Tim was the natural and fairly obvious choice to resume his role with The Vapors when they reformed and had joined us in the Shoreham pub pre-gig after completing load-in, build and sound checking duties.

Tim has many memories of his own, of course, but as they come not from a fan's view, but the perspective of the band's longest serving technical companion and his roadie life, it would be thoroughly disappointing if they didn't include at least some tales of rock and roll excess, and he doesn't disappoint in this respect.

It's not quite TV sets being thrown out of windows, but he does recall a night in a Scarborough hotel with various band members jumping, elevated parasols in hand, Mary Poppins style, from their hotel window into the swimming pool.

The long US tours were apparently kept competitive with the "Holiday Inn Olympics" featuring an on-the-road series of athletics trials that included leaping on to the sideboard at the end of the bed, somersaulting off it and bouncing off the bed in order to kick the picture off the wall in one sleek, gymnastic movement.

Slightly more mysteriously, Tim recalls what was probably the first evening the band spent out in New York City. "It was me, Steve and Howard. Ed too maybe. There was this guy sat at the end of the bar by himself, didn't say anything. He was on the well-dressed side of shifty, smart suit, that kind of thing, and there was us bunch of hooligans from England at the other end of the bar." After a while, the barman informed the group that the guy at the end of the bar was buying them all a drink. "We said thanks," continues Tim, "and then soon after he got up and left. The barman asked us if we knew who he was, and when we told him we didn't, he just said 'Oh, he's a hitman from the mafia.'"

It's hardly Keith Moon or Ronnie Wood stuff, but it's good to know there is a proper history of Vapors-appropriate level rock and roll tour mayhem.

A group of us, Tim included, crowded round Elaine's organised and chronological treasure trove of photos and memories from the time and gazed in wonder as each turn of the page starkly re-visualised specific memories that each and every one of us had cherished for so long. The photographs provided the strongest memory jolters, as people began to recognise 35-year-old pictures of themselves. It became apparent that not only must Elaine have been present at so many of the same evenings as Kev, Colin and I, but judging by the angles of some of her photographs we must have been stood pretty much next to each other all those years previously. People began recounting their own memories of the same events, and their anecdotes triggered other memories in others, and it began to feel like the happiest school reunion of all time, encompassing all the joyful reminiscing without having to include any of the dreaded recollections of school itself.

Inevitably, conversation turned to a roundtable "Do you remember someone called... Whatever happened to... Who was that guy/girl..." free for all. The core of the group had met up a few times now, and we all had our long-lost gig buddies, those that hadn't turned up at the reunion shows, or contributed to the Facebook page, about whom we were curious. For us, of course, it was Sarah and the glove puppet girls, and for the first time I voiced openly my surprise that Sarah had not surfaced. Of all of us, she was probably the biggest Vapors fan of them all, and her even then media-savvy and worldly outlook made it surprising that she hadn't turned up at least online at some point. Rob remembered Sarah, the fact of his previous meeting with us already having been evidenced by his production of that Frantic Aardvarks badge. As we discussed people, and gigs, I began to realise that I did indeed remember Rob, not from Vapors gigs, but from countless London pub performances from a post-Vapors gig favourite of both Sarah and I, The Gymslips. Rob, however, was no wiser than me as to her whereabouts.

Scrapbook exhausted and stage time approaching, we made our way over to the venue. The Ropetackle Arts Centre is a modern, purpose-built arts and music space with a large, comfortable lobby bar and an acoustically obliging performance space. We entered through the bar, Owen's compulsive collector side immediately getting the better of him as he headed to the large glass fronted window that opens the space up to Shoreham High Street to snaffle the evening's promotional poster. Immediately spotted by one of the venue's eagle-eyed, volunteer, librarian-like front of house staff and asked politely whether he was "authorised to remove that poster" he grinned a sheepish, guilty look of a mischievous schoolboy getting rumbled and admitted that he probably wasn't. He has since returned to Sussex but for a while was undoubtedly on the wanted list in parts of the Adur and Worthing district.

The gig was another good one, my sister was delighted to see the songs she'd had no choice but to ingest word for word, note by note when she was 11 or 12 being brought alive, recounting her enforced absorption of his songs to Dave after the show, much to his seemingly genuine amusement. Even her chilled out, reggae loving partner enjoyed it, and all in all the evening was ticked off by all and sundry as another great success.

Cold Wet Forehead

A summer break followed, and having decided not to travel to Blackpool, my next scheduled Vapors gig was the one booked for a small pub venue, The Thunderbolt, in Bristol, in early September. I was looking forward to this for personal reasons, with it happening to coincide perfectly with the week my youngest son was due to move into his first-year student accommodation at Bristol's University of the West of England. We arranged to travel down on the Saturday for the gig, leaving his worldly possessions stashed in the car whilst we spent the weekend in a hotel and he got to discover his new hometown, before I transitioned to the proud but emotional parental role when we moved him in on the Monday. It's a truly momentous time in a parent's life, taking a child to see their boyhood heroes for the first time, and I was looking forward to it hugely. Oh yeah, and the dropping him at University thing too, of course.

Unfortunately events overtook me, and I became ill whilst on holiday in Crete with a bunch of pub mates, pretty much falling off the aeroplane on my return to Gatwick and heading straight to A & E at the Royal Sussex County Hospital, thanks to my wife agreeing to pick me up from the airport. She took one glance at me with a face composed equally of sympathy and a "Look at the state of you" sense of disbelief before spending 30 minutes piloting me south on the A23 laying out exactly what was going to happen next. Two months in various hospital wards ensued, within the manic conglomeration of patched up Victorian buildings, hastily constructed extensions, portacabins and tower blocks that comprise the site and are somehow shoehorned into a woefully inadequate inner-city position just back from the sea in Kemp Town. I remember very little about the first few days I was there, other than occasionally waking up whilst strapped to all sorts of beeping devices and intravenous drips, and being wheeled on trolleys down endless corridors between wards, and off for various inspections, X-rays, MRI scans and all sorts of other mysterious probing and prodding. The week ended with surgery, removing certain by now dead, seriously infected and dangerous to retain extremities, and whilst it would be a week or two before I had the seriousness of the state I had been in explained to me, I began to recover. A couple of days after that first operation I began to regain some normal level of awareness and began to realise that life was going to be slightly different from here on in.

For a while there was a risk that I would lose the lower half of my right leg to amputation, and clearly that required some mental adjustment. The process of slowly coming to terms with how thorough my lifestyle revisions would need to be from that point forward, for ever, as well as the concerns about whether I would be able to continue earning a living in the way I was accustomed, obviously occupied my mind. But clearly worse than any of this, as I regained awareness of (and indeed sight of) the world around me both physically and metaphorically, was the jolt of frustrated adrenaline that surged through me very early one morning at the sudden realisation that at home, in my top drawer, was a bunch of gig tickets that I wouldn't be able to put to use. There were the Vapors ones, of course, including that much anticipated Bristol one that was happening that very evening, but there were many others too. If The Vapors had reawakened a teenage passion within me in terms of habitual attendance at their shows, that passion in turn had re-engendered an enthusiasm to take in any band I possibly could, be they on the long-worn comeback trail themselves, newcomers, or indeed old-timers that had never been away. I had tickets for forthcoming shows by Interpol, The Happy Mondays, The Libertines and The Psychedelic Furs amongst others and they were all going to have to be consigned to the dustbin with The Vapors ones for Bristol, Salisbury, London and Portmeirion. Disaster.

The reality is that I had been lucky. The rest of the year was spent in and out of hospital, both in Brighton and in the comparative luxury of a specialist unit in East Grinstead, and the end result prognosis was that I'd probably make a full recovery. I'd certainly have to modify the way I lived my life to ensure that the recovery remained sustainable, and undoubtedly, I'd probably walk a bit funny from that point on, but it was going to be OK. In fact, two years later, I'm still saddled with a non-healing wound and infected bones that still pose a danger and I'm currently awaiting further surgery that in all likelihood will result in the same outcome as that which I was at risk of two years ago. But if it draws a line under things for once and for all then that will get me to where I need to be, which actually feels like a big cause for optimism. My glass is considerably more than half-full, and with the exception of having to do things in slow motion a lot of the time, life is good and normal, and in actual fact I feel physically better than I had done for years, without ever realising that I wasn't well.

By early 2018 I had recovered sufficiently to begin tentative returns to work, and to normality, and to paying bills, and to travelling on buses (driving an adapted vehicle was a year away yet), and to all of life's trivialities. As a result, and of far greater consequence, my thoughts turned to the far grander momentousness of how I could plot the wheres and whens of my return to live music events.

The calendar was kind, with a certain recently reformed early 80s band that had originally hailed from Guildford booking a show at Nell's Jazz and Blues Club in West Kensington for March. Nell's itself does not share quite the same heritage as the other London venues whose stage the band had graced since they reconvened, but nevertheless it does form an important modern Vapors piece of history as it was the location, in the 1990s and then known as The Orange Club, where Steve, whilst working there as a sound engineer, met his now partner Sally, who was managing the establishment.

Nestled across the Cromwell Road from the club, next to West Kensington Station, however, is a venue that conversely is steeped in tradition. Although now a fairly formulaic London Sports Bar, The Famous Three Kings plies its business in the building that was formerly The Nashville, another mainstay of that left-hand live ads NME page in the late 70s, and where The Vapors had indeed performed first time round. A fairly obvious location for pre-gig drinks, we began to drift towards the pub from our various nationwide locations from about 5.00pm onwards.

I was expecting it to be an emotional night, but I was genuinely overwhelmed by the welcome I received from so many, most of whom I'd known for a maximum of eighteen months, who suddenly felt like they were serious lifelong friends, and some of whom undoubtedly now will be. Beccy joined us, having travelled up from Brighton whilst I had travelled up from Devon after one of many convalescent trips to my mother's, and I recall a blur of hugs and best wishes and of holding back the tears, which would have been a perfect night out in itself, except there was a Vapors gig to come at the end of it as well. It's the little things, as they say, and Branka's posting on Facebook the following day of a picture of some of us in the pub with a simple caption stating that it was "So great to have Mike back in the fold" did finally cause the holding back of the tears to fail, as had, months previously whilst I was still in hospital, the receipt of a get well card from all of the band sent when they learned why I had gone AWOL from gig attendance and the regular posting of Facebook nonsense for a while.

A couple of fans who I'd not even met before but who were clearly fitting the simple Vapors Family requirements template left the pub early to grab me a seat at one of the few tables splattered sparsely at the front of the slightly raised area of the venue above the main dance floor (thanks Weston!). We ended up sat together for the evening, discussing the inevitably similar but always different at the periphery musical memories from our youth. The band played, Beccy went forward for a dance and I did my best to stay seated but ended up leaning on the rail that separated our platform from the main floor, prompting Branka, for the first of several hundred times, to remind me to take care of myself, whilst I reminded her, for the first of several hundred times, that she wasn't my fucking mother. Owen left halfway through the gig, having been forced into an impossible dilemma that his poor head couldn't unscramble, that posed by The Vapors playing on the same night as The Stranglers. To quote one of the latter's earlier classic songs, he did the only thing possible, hotfooting it to Brixton on the tube, where he would have us believe that he arrived in time for the end of their set. Back at Nell's it was, of course, over far too quickly.

I don't recall much of the band's performance to be honest. There were a couple of additional new numbers, a slight rearrangement of what had largely become the staple set since Dublin, and all of the usual favourites. But that night they could have played the whole lot on out of tune kazoos and improvised instruments made out of tea-chests and string, sung them all backwards in Mongolian and I wouldn't have cared. I was there, so was that little guy singing with the stripy shirt on, that left-handed bass-slinging rock of stability and confidence, and that still permanently beaming drummer. It was also the first time that I had got to see Dan performing the lead guitar duties, his previous appearances off the bench having come at three of the gigs I had elected to miss the previous summer, and there was something quite inspirational about seeing him doing so with such skill and obvious enjoyment alongside his father.

This time a fully conscious decision was made, and the complete, final reversion to teenage obsession was deliberately arrived at. I pledged to myself in a life's too short moment of reflection that, never knowing when the band, or indeed I, might come to a sudden end, it would have to take a very special reason for me to miss any more of their gigs. Ever. Anywhere.

A return to Norwich followed, on campus in the leafy surrounds of the University of East Anglia on a beautiful spring day, where the band were supporting Buzzcocks, a band I hadn't seen for years, and a gig that, with hindsight, I am so glad I attended following the sad news of Pete Shelley's death later in the year.

A trip to Manchester was next, with the support comprising the farewell performance of Dan's University band, Rothman Jack, and a cross country trip to Newcastle for a gig the following night. All of us have our personal favourite Vapors gigs since (and before) Dublin of course. Newcastle became, and possibly remains, at least from the perspective of the band's playing that night, mine. A warm summer's evening spent outside a pub, separated only from the venue, The Cluny, by a small, slightly wooded green space, itself occupied by people socialising over a drink purchased from The Cluny's own bar, all built on an atmospheric steep slope in a regenerated area running down to the River Tyne, was a perfect start. With the company including a number of the Vapors Family's northern branch, who I was equally as pleased to see after so long and who were equally as affable as the Nell's pre-gig crowd had been, it just got better. My wannabe surrogate mother Branka plonked me on a seat behind the merch stall for the gig, for which I was actually quite grateful but of course did my best to protest about, which in turn gave me a perfect view over a boisterous, noisy Geordie crowd. The band played a blistering set, in my opinion bettering anything that had gone before both technically and in terms of plain feel good atmosphere.

Despite my newly avowed statement of intent, the following night's gig in Scotland was still one too many for me at that point so I headed south in the morning safe in the knowledge that there was another gig, in Birmingham, coming up soon. Kev flew over from Germany for that one, which many people I speak to insist at least matched the Newcastle gig in quality terms, although for me it was unfortunately less memorable due to not feeling quite so fit and well that night, and having to sit at the back with no stage view. That wasn't a great problem in all honesty, it was part of my new reality and I was still just glad to be there. Additionally, it gave me the chance to spend the evening chatting to TV Smith, who had played an acoustic support slot, and for whom Branka clearly had a middle aged crush hung over from teenage days and which caused her to give me amused fake dagger looks all evening as I chatted away with him whilst she was unable to flirt with him herself on account of her husband being on stage in front of us all.

As in the previous year, I opted not to travel to Blackpool for the Rebellion Festival, but three weeks after that the lads appeared in something akin to a circus tent erected in a forest in Sussex one afternoon as part of the somewhat away-from-the-norm Byline Festival. A pleasant summer's afternoon was spent in a field, drinking beer with the band before Department S, and then The Members, and then The Vapors themselves, delivered their sets. This all happened a few hours after a weird ten minutes in a Land Rover on the way from the car park to the festival site. Owen had picked me up at Haywards Heath station and we fortuitously arrived in the car park at the same time as the band, who were assured someone would be on hand to help them get their equipment to the distant tented stage.

Help dutifully arrived, and as I accepted her insistence on this occasion without protest, Branka persuaded the driver to allow me to accompany their guitars and equipment in the passenger seat as we began the slow, bumpy trek across some fields whilst she, the others, and the band all slogged it on foot.

"So which band are you then?" the driver asked me amiably.

"Well, I'm just here as a fan, you know…" I replied, equally amiably, "but they're The Vapors."

"Oh ok, what sort of music do you play?"

"Well like I say, I'm not in the band, but they're a guitar band, new wave, you know, that sort of thing."

Persevering, he continued, "So would I know any of your songs?"

"Their songs"

"Sorry?"

"Well you'd probably know one of their songs."

"Oh great, what's that then?"

"Turning Japanese."

"Oh! I love that one! Did you write it?"

My amiability had turned to mild, and then raised, and then excessive irritation as I replied "Well, Dave did, he was one of the guys in the car park, one of the band, the band that I've told you about three times I'm not actually in."

"Oh!" he exclaimed, "Clever Dave! So anyway, what instrument do you play then?"

Fortunately we arrived backstage before I was forced to crack open one of the guitars and demonstrate my incompetence to him to such an extent that he got the point, but I did spend the rest of the afternoon harbouring a slight concern that he'd watch the set, notice I wasn't a part of it, and sling me off site for being some kind of fraudulent lift-blagger. It did cross my mind to ask Michael if perhaps I should deputise on drums for the night just in case but decided that was probably a non-starter.

The lads played a relatively short, festival-style set, and we decided against hanging around for the rest of the talent on display that evening, which included such diverse non-attractions to our refined musical ears as The Blow Monkeys and Pussy Riot, and Owen dropped me home. I was tucked up in bed by 10.30pm. My kind of festival.

Another high-quality performance followed a couple of weeks later in Cambridge, one of the strongest memories of which I have was a heart-warming few minutes after the show when Sally brought her daughter around to the front of the auditorium, wide-eyed and full of excitement at her dad's performance. Steve joined us whilst the late-night unconditional outpouring of praise for her father was still in full flow, his face swept with a show of parental love and pride. I was still running quite high on a surfeit of emotional relief as I continued to recover from my illness and continued to tick off Vapors gigs. As a result, the moment was such a wonderful confirmation of how, nearly 40 years later, here we all were, doing what we'd all always done, and loving every minute of it, but with the benefit and hindsight of having successfully negotiated happy paths through life along the way.

2016 had seen a return of my special band, one that in reality could have gone either way, but one that turned out to be triumphant, uplifting, promising and positive in equal measures. 2017 had built on that, the promise had grown and the growing number amongst a loosely attached but bonded forever ensemble of fans and friends gathered pace. And the spring and summer of 2018 felt like the crowning glory, with packed gigs and high-quality performances that just improved as they went along.

It was difficult to see how there was any conceivable way that things could possibly get any better.

Silver Machines

Things got even better.

Since the reunion, there had been a growing clamour in the US for the band to return to the country where their popularity had, in many ways, exceeded the levels it reached in the UK back in 1980. The demand grew, with increasing numbers of fans joining the Facebook fans' group, aware of what had been happening in the UK, and desperately requesting some US gigs with ever greater levels of enthusiasm and desire. The band were forced regularly to explain just how much they'd love to, but how difficult it would be for a group with no label backing and no links to local promoters or organisations to make the trip. Coupled with the realistic costs of equipment transportation and the permits that would be required to allow them simply to perform, it seemed that there were, unfortunately, simply too many obstacles.

Towards the end of 2017, one of the Internet's more positive innovations, coupled with some dogged local heroism from some soon to be American members of The Vapors Family, came into play.

Enter lifelong Vapors fan Evan Blonder.

In 2016, Evan had heard from a Podcast in the US that Dave was putting the band back together. Sensing his chance may finally have come, he followed with interest as the first four gigs were announced and became such successes and noted the following spring's 100 Club gig being announced. "The girl I'm dating now, Antoinette, she's a go-getter, she's older than me but she has so much energy and I figured she'd want to come to London and see them so I just said 'Why don't we go to London to see them?'" he explains. "She was like 'You wanna go to London to see The Vapors?' and she was like 'Nah…'" As a result, Evan held off, but the more he thought about it, the more he was determined, so he resolved to travel over by himself, but by the time he'd made this decision the gig was sold out.

He began to think that he'd never get to see the band, but at the end of the year he finally made it, to the show at the 229 in London in November. "This time I just said, 'I'm going' and Antoinette was like 'Yeah OK I'll come to London with you, but I've been there so many times can we do something else as well?' So we made a trip to Amsterdam and then flew to London."

He'd got there, and he made all the necessary contacts in advance, having already got in touch with Shaun to sound out the possibility of US dates but always receiving the same response outlining the sheer costs and impracticality of putting all the arrangements together.

Evan joined the pre-gig meet up in the pub, and rubbed his eyes in disbelief as, 37 years after buying a record in New York City as a way of impressing a girlfriend, he finally got to see The Vapors. "They put me in the spotlight in front of Dave and I was namechecked, just wow! That was kind of Full Circle for me" he reminisces, describing a return to teenage emotions that I was already so familiar with. Antoinette provided an Americanised version of my wife's own observations concerning the front of stage audience behaviour with a yelled "Why are you doing this? You're fucking grown men! I'm going to stand over there!", requiring Evan to retreat slightly in order to offer her the required degree of protection. Nevertheless, she too enjoyed watching the band, as well as the audience, in the same way that my wife has done at any of the latter-day gigs that she has herself attended.

He admits to being overwhelmed when he finally got to meet the band after the show, and even more bewildered when he felt a tug on his arm and Shaun asked if they could have a chat. "I'm like, this is crazy, the manager of The Vapors wants to talk to me?" Shaun stated simply, I would assume in the one-speed no-nonsense way with which he addresses every practicality, that "We're ready to bring the band to the US, what can we do?"

Staggered but elated, Evan thought out loud and said that he wasn't sure how they could kick things off, but he was at least able to confirm his certainty that there would be a big fanbase ready to go to shows. All he could suggest immediately was that he knew some people, who knew some people. And then he hit on the idea of creating a GoFundMe online fundraising campaign for fans on the Internet, and the seeds were sown.

Back home, he set up the page, came up with some ideas as to how to attract fans' pledges with packaged premium offers such as the ability to play with the band at soundchecks when they finally got there, signed T-shirts and posters, "Vapors experiences" involving hanging out with the band pre-gig, and all sorts of price-ranged enticements. There was no pressure for fans to pledge any particular amount, a single dollar would do, but if they had more to spend, the packages would provide some rewards for the fans' money, which in turn would feed the growing US hunger for the band to return there after 38 years and indeed make possible the band's great desire to play there.

"We set the page up, I showed it to Shaun, he made some adjustments, we put it up live, and literally watched the money start to roll in" he states, in a half nonchalant, half wild with childlike disbelief way. The packages began to be snapped up very quickly, in one case to Evan's equal delight and disappointment when "The day with the band one went before I could get it!", but unperturbed he made the next best pledge he could and snapped up one of the soundcheck deals for himself.

Attention turned to the practicalities. Venue selection had included consideration of some iconic New York City concert halls. The Bowery and The Irving Plaza were considered, as was the smaller Red Lion in Greenwich Village, before The Mercury Lounge on the Lower East Side was decided upon. "We were looking for a place that we could definitely sell out," Evan explains, "I thought they could do better, a bigger venue, but Shaun said 'No we gotta test it out first time round' and we settled on The Mercury Lounge because the ownership were really interested and responsive, they wanted to know what we actually wanted to do and so on, and they had the scope to put on three consecutive nights."

Within a matter of weeks, along with a few other cash boosts, the required amount of money had been pledged via the GoFundMe website, amongst which was a significant sum from UK fans who, like myself, had pledged some funds with the vague notion that we may fly over to the gigs, but that even if we didn't we were helping the band who had done so much for us in the preceding 18 months. "I wanted to continue, to raise some more to really show how much interest there was," Evan continues, "but Shaun was happy with the amount, so we went ahead at that point and attention turned to the logistics."

In the UK, Shaun focused on the not inconsiderable task of obtaining performance visas for the band, and to drawing up the contracts, and the deals got signed and two of the gigs were initially announced. Unsurprisingly, I couldn't resist, and bought tickets for both immediately I was able, using the priority booking status my pledge to the campaign had afforded me, as did a number of my UK fan friends. The remainder of the tickets immediately went on public sale, and immediately sold out, and the third gig was immediately added, and in turn also immediately sold out.

Back in the US, attention turned to finer detail. The venue would provide PA and sound equipment, the band would bring their own personal favoured and treasured guitars on the plane, and certain small usual "gig comfort" constituents that the band used may need to be compromised. There were, however, other requirements that, whilst they wouldn't be taken for granted in the UK, and would require due attention and ticking off, necessitated a lot more effort in the case of gigs taking place 3500 miles away.

Up stepped Bobby Weiss.

Evan recalls his learning of the band's restart in calm, measured tones. Bobby, on the other hand, is more animated. "I'd still not really ever found out what happened to the band" he explains, "but then, finally, one day, I discovered that fans' Facebook page." Not only had he found the page, he found it at the right time. "It was right around the time of that Half Moon thing when Dave got up on stage with Ed to join Steve" he continues, "and I just flipped out man! I fell off my fucking chair and rubbed my eyes. I just couldn't believe what I was seeing!"

Bobby spent weeks after his discovery getting up to speed with events in the UK and reaching out to any number of people already on that Facebook page just to converse about all things Vapors. "I got connected to Branka and Dave and just got chatting about how, like I've said to you, it was that band that got me playing" he continues, explaining how, like it had done for many of us, music had taken a back seat whilst young children were raised. But that now he was back playing again with his own band, Pajamazon, which also features his son Jack amongst the line-up. Bobby had sent the Fentons a YouTube link to one of his own band's songs, "Baby Tee", which in his words is "definitely inspired by Spring Collection." To his amazement they sent him a home shot mobile phone video of the pair of them listening to, and loving, his music. "I lost my fucking mind!" he laughs. "Surreal and mind-blowing. For 35 years I wondered what happened to this guy, the guy who inspired me to play, and now here he is loving my song! I sent them Pajamazon CDs, they sent me T-shirts and badges from the first UK shows, it was just incredible."

Bobby watched as the reunion unfolded and joined the clamour stateside for a band return to the US, and then "All of a sudden Evan started the GoFundMe page and I was suddenly like 'oh my god this is going to happen!'"

Aware of Bobby's musical presence in New York State, and already considering the offer of a support slot on one of the gig nights, Shaun got in touch with Bobby via email and asked him if his band would like to play. "Well…I thought about it" he laughs, "but whilst there was clearly only going to be one answer it still seemed completely unreal." He was then able to help with all those nitty-gritty details that just couldn't be handled from the UK, working with Evan after Shaun had put them in touch for the first time. He arranged for the provision of such essentials as backup amps and equipment, a spare left-handed bass for Steve, and crucially a set of roto-toms for the drum kit Michael would be using, required due to the band having decided to include a couple of songs from the Magnets album, more popular in America than the UK, that would require their use.

October came around. Two years after I'd boarded a plane from Gatwick enroute to see The Vapors in a significant upgrade to any modes of travel used to reach any of their previous gigs, I was about to do so again. This time, however, it was no short hop flight over to Ireland. This time it was a full-blown long-haul affair. No matter how frequent a traveller one is, I defy anyone not to feel at least some extra tingle of anticipation and a little sniff of glamour when about to board a giant transatlantic airliner. And here I was, about to do that, as Shaun was to drolly remark a few months later, in the company of a band that had become my first real teenage obsession so long ago, on the way to New York City to watch them play three sold out gigs.

I met Owen and Jacquie at the check-in desk, along with Dave, Branka, Steve, Sally, Michael, Dan and his girlfriend Kat. Tim Cox and his wife Mandy arrived, as did Shaun Modern and Jacqui Carroll. There was an expectant excitement, somewhere between the feel of a long weekend away with a bunch of pub mates emanating from some of us, and an equally excited, but slightly more undefinable mix of anticipation and uncertainty emanating from the band. Bags checked in, the necessary but precisely managed and impeccably planned check-in of the band's guitars was then supervised by Shaun, with flight cases being doublechecked and cling-film being wrapped tightly around them as the final layer of protection, both physically, and psychologically in the minds of the instruments' owners. Someone pointed out that nobody would really want to traipse round the shops of New York looking for further cling-film to shroud the cases for the return flight, so, having no other baggage to take on board, Jacquie offered to carry the bulky roll that was still largely intact as hand luggage.

Security negotiated, we settled into a bar for a drink and discussed our expectations, gig-related and tourism-related alike. We were joined in the departure lounge by Rob Payne, who had checked in later than us, and boarded the plane for what was a relatively pain-free and comfortable flight.

Arriving at JFK and its customary queues to get through immigration, it was now 3.00am the following day UK time, and unsurprisingly we were all getting tired, especially those (mentioning no names) who had used the eight hour flight as an extension of the drinking session that had started at Gatwick. The band were travelling on special visas allowing them to perform in the US, and as we went through as a group, once one set of questions had been painstakingly answered by our self-nominated spokesperson, Branka Fenton, the rest of us were ushered through relatively quickly. I glanced wearily towards the baggage reclaim, peering at screens to see if I could identify where to go, but as I did so I caught sight of the top half of a giant roll of cling-film bobbling up and down as it was marched through the hall, so we were able to follow Jacquie from afar and become reunited with our luggage.

We exited customs and were met by the man without whom none of us would have been there, Evan Blonder. Evan had no need for one of those signs people hold up at airports proclaiming "The Vapors" because he was proudly wearing one of the band's new merchandising T-shirts that had been specially produced for the weekend's events.

It was a great gesture by Evan to meet us late at night, navigate us through the myriad identikit terminal buildings and faceless concrete miles of JFK Airport's transit system, and then to help us wait for and board our hotel's shuttle bus, before going the extra mile and helping us with our bags and making absolutely sure that we had all checked in OK. But it pales into insignificance against the monumental achievement he set out to achieve, and succeeded in executing, just to get the band there in the first place.

It may have been nothing more than a faceless, transitory, 24-hour practical airport hotel, but the bar still had neon Bud signs illuminating its interior and wise-cracking single guys sat on barstools drinking from bottles. We grabbed a large table surrounded by felted, purple seats and sat down. We were in America.

The band have always referred fondly to their memories of touring the US, and from the Facebook page alone it was already obvious how many people were excited about this return. But as we sat down for the last beers of a very long day, Evan wore his excitement, enthusiasm and passion for the band not so much on his sleeve but rather running down his arms and all over the rest of us. Here was a guy who had begun a labour of love a few months previously, and who had succeeded, in some style, in achieving the original aim. In doing so he must have put a fair old slog in, and once things began to come to fruition, must have given up a lot of his own time to organise and smooth things through. But here he was, another fan with a Vapors memory or two to share, a friendly story to recount with all, and all with that slightly more fervent demeanour and fanaticism that the British perceive in all Americans. I began to understand already why the band had always spoken so affectionately of their times in the US, and the fans they had met, where they had always played to larger audiences than they had ever mustered in the UK.

The airport stop was for one night only, with Lower East Side hotels booked for the remainder of the stay within walking distance of the venue. An early start was required for the band, with a further minibus booked, and Shaun's military martialling ensured that all went to schedule. Owen, Jacquie and I took the softer option, preferring a long sleep, a late lazy breakfast and a cab ride into Manhattan. Refreshed and awake, as we neared that unmistakable skyline set against a crisp, autumnal blue sky and crossed the Williamsburg Bridge, we planned our day ahead.

We checked in to The Holiday Inn, chosen in preference to the band's hotel due to it being slightly closer to the venue, and directly above a subway station. We were not planning to sit still whilst in town.

Immediately heading out to explore our surroundings, locate the venue and acquire some increasingly necessary caffeine, we wandered around the blocks stretching out to the north-west of the hotel. The area, on the northern tip of the Lower East Side, is typical of many Manhattan neighbourhoods, simultaneously down at heel and gentrified, with street dwellers and trendy coffee bars in equal measures. The blocks are full of themed bars, cafes and street outlets selling international food of myriad styles and an even wider quality span, boutique shops, tatty corner stores and delis, and any number of other outlets, whose purpose wasn't always clear, and whose owners probably didn't care. In the fifteen minutes it took us to walk the three blocks up to East Houston Street, and our first sight of The Mercury Lounge, we passed schools, front yards with laundry strung out across them and young children playing, churches, shops, unknown purpose metal-shuttered establishments, boarded up buildings, bustling building sites, parks and all the people, so many people. Reminding ourselves where we were wasn't necessary, but if it had been, all we would have needed to do was look upwards at the rows of tenement blocks, some in need of some repair, some beautifully resplendent with their gleaming refurbished brickwork, all clad with their seemingly summit-less external Jack-and-the-Beanstalk fire escapes, many still topped off with the once mandatory New York City water towers.

Despite my previous scorn for Kev's insistence on visiting the venue the night before the Dublin gig, and despite the fact that we all had our tickets for all three gigs safely hidden away in our hotel safes, there was something that was genuinely electrifying when the setting for the following three nights' adventures came into view. We did all that we could do, which was to stare at it for a bit and take photos of each other standing in front of the signage, before remembering that we were fully grown adults and that our time would be better spent acquiring what was by now even more urgently vital caffeine.

We meandered along the wide open but traffic heavy expanse of East Houston Street, and settled into Remedy, a classic New York diner with towering bar stools set at a long, solid bar for those wanting a drink or a snack. There were all shapes and sizes of table set for people of all shapes and sizes, circular sofa-style padded seating for those seeking a longer and more relaxed experience, huge glass windows, a tiled floor laid out with giant brown and cream diamonds, lights and more lights, and loud, attentive, wise-cracking waiters. We didn't know it at the time, but this place would become the brunch basecamp for a significant number of the whole UK touring party over the weekend, but for now we satisfied the caffeine cravings and had a light lunch.

We kept track with the remainder of the British contingent who were flying out that day. Matt Inskip with his girlfriend Sarah, Elaine Bevan and Jane Wadman arrived from Heathrow. Dave's nephew Jim and his family hit town, and Rich Stevenson, from Sheffield, arrived on a flight from Manchester with his then partner and the pair of them checked into the same hotel as the three of us. Graham and Karen Ivey, who technically had the shortest distance to travel as the crow flies, as they live in deepest Cornwall, arrived after Karen had taken a convoluted route across England to Norwich to visit her daughter and a newly arrived grandchild and back to Heathrow for the flight.

Everyone had their plans for that first evening; for the band that meant taking it easy whilst under Shaun's close, watchful, schoolmasterly eye, whilst for Owen, Jacquie and myself it meant a night out at another of New York's legendary music venues, the Irving Plaza, where it just so happened that The Damned were playing.

I'd been to gigs in New York before, and I'd seen British acts play there; however this would be the first time that I'd seen a band with whom I was so familiar play in the US. It's fair to say that Damned audiences are slightly unlike any other in the UK, so I was curious to see what the US equivalent would be, and how they behaved. The building that hosts the venue is over 150 years old, was converted into a ballroom in the 1920s, and only opened as a rock venue in 1978, however the interior feels like a slice of Victoriana. Once inside, you could be forgiven from appearances' sake at least for thinking that you were in London. A wooden clad downstairs array of cosy snug seating areas, cloakrooms and toilets gives way to a long, straight staircase leading to the main auditorium, a rectangular all standing room capable of housing just over 1000 people. Surrounding the room is a small balcony area, bars at the back completing the archetypal rock venue, and acoustically it's a great place to see bands.

The place filled up, and the crowd turned out to be pretty similar to that which would attend a UK equivalent. It was largely male, largely white, largely jeans and t-shirted, and largely middle-aged, but with a higher than average number of green-haired fifty and sixty-somethings in shorts, combat trousers or leathers, and there were safety pins aplenty and regulation tattoos and piercings. There were also a higher than usual number of well dressed, younger college types, but other than that we really could have been in London. The band shuffled on, with the unique British-ness of the theme tune to "It Ain't Half Hot Mum" bellowing from the PA.

"Meet the gang cos the boys are here" sang along the three of us at the tops of our voices, to our great delight, and the complete bemusement of everyone around us. As Captain Sensible and Co. picked up their instruments and a cool, shade sporting, black leather glove wearing, pale faced, greased backed haired Dave Vanian glided, ever more vampire-like, on to the stage, we were reminded audibly of our location as the whoops, whistles and shouted "Yeeeaaahhh"s of the crowd accompanied their arrival. The British sense of reserve can sometimes lead to a smug and not always unjustified mild sense of scorn when witnessing a bunch of excited Americans, but the enthusiasm and unbridled enjoyment it openly belies in the context of a rock gig is difficult not to embrace. As well as savouring the moment, my thoughts turned to how this level of energy would feel on the following three nights, when directed at The Vapors.

The Damned played a storming set. It was the first time I'd seen them in a while, and this gig, like a couple of others of theirs I have been at in the UK since, saw them playing as well as I think they have ever done over their long lifetime. And they've done it without 35 years off in the middle, so all credit to them.

Mood switched to permanent high and seemingly set in for several days like a high-pressure weather system, we headed back to the hotel, primed and ready for the main event, which began the following day.

With all members of the UK fraternity now settled in and rested, the Friday followed a pattern that was to be set for the weekend. With no particular structure, groups of us would meet up and head off to one or more of the attractions

Manhattan has to offer, do the general tourist thing awhile, and then, in different groups, assemble for our disparate pre-gig activities. For the band, of course, that meant setting up, sound checking and preparing. For the fans, well you can take the Vapors Family out of the UK, but you can't change their habits, so a venue for the pre-gig meet-up was established, and a general invite issued via Facebook for US fans to join us.

We settled on Benson's, a Craft beer outlet immediately around the corner from The Mercury Lounge. Small, New York trendy but in a relaxed not painful way, with wooden floors, a big glass frontage, bar stools and high tables aplenty, it was immediately and obviously perfect. Easy for people to come and go and eat and drink as they pleased, we quickly got to know the owners and warned them that we'd be a permanent fixture for the next three evenings. They must have been well used to pre-gig audiences frequenting their bar early evenings, but nevertheless were engagingly welcoming, genuinely interested to hear our tale and frankly amazed at how many of us had made the trip from the UK. Within one round they remembered what each of us was drinking, and continued to do so for the rest of the weekend, making some of us feel more welcome in there than we had done in several years of some of the UK pubs that some of us could recall having used as our locals in the past.

We were joined by a handful of US fans, and the story-swapping and camaraderie of pre-Vapors gig meetups went truly global.

Immediately before we settled in Benson's for the first time, I had paid a solo visit on the way from the hotel to the local branch of McDonald's for the sole purpose of acquiring a photo of a McDonald's Apple Pie to send to Colin as my way of saying "Wish you were here" with a very old Vapors memory for us both. Fortunately, it cost very little, a good thing as it was consigned to the bin before it could do any damage.

This story is full of superlatives from start to end, but the remainder of the evening, and the repeat runs on the following two nights, were like nothing in the gig world some of us had ever undergone before, and I'd honestly be hard pushed to dream up a scenario that could ever surpass them.

I've Got Your Picture

We wandered around the corner from Benson's to see a crowd of people milling around the entrance, including an uncharacteristically nervous Branka, puffing away on her electronic cigarette. She saw me coming and grabbed me in order to introduce the guy she was chatting to, Bobby Weiss.

Medium sized, shaven headed and wearing a perma-grin Bobby shook my hand enthusiastically and we chatted like long lost friends who had never met before, not quite sure which one of us was the most delighted just to be there. The tone for the company I'd be keeping for the next three nights had been set before I'd even ventured into the venue.

In through the door, past an equally friendly doorman who was to become a constant source of amusement with his quips over the next couple of nights due to his proximity to the merch stall which became a kind of regular rendezvous point during each of the shows, and the room entered out into a long, thin corridor-like bar leading ultimately to the auditorium. I went and checked out the main room, small stage set at the far end, darkly lit with sound desk at the rear next to the entrance door, and a handful of sofa-like seats down the left-hand side. For the second night running it felt like I'd entered a perfect, fitted to some kind of atmospheric new wave venue blueprint, London music club, that just happened to be set in New York City. And for the second time, the difference was the slight, but discernible higher level of anticipation, hype and general whooping that comes with being a part of an American audience.

There were two support bands, local New Jersey based rock outfit The Mylars, and The Split Squad, both with an impressive member biography. The Split Squad's, particularly, is hard to match, and would be even harder to make up, featuring former members of Blondie (drummer Clem Burke, the old pal of Evan's former bandmate), The Plimsouls and (the clincher) the in-stadium organ player for the Boston Red Sox, and the band's singer and bassist Michael Giblin. They had supported The Vapors at a couple of UK gigs earlier in the year, so were known to UK fans and band alike. I drifted in and out of the auditorium during both bands' sets, sharing my time chatting to the UK contingent and an ever increasing number of US fans as we mingled in the hall, and the bar, and the merch stand, in what felt like a massive party with no real need to wait for introductions before chatting to someone. Most, of course, had their own Vapors story to tell, but the outpouring of new ones, from the stateside perspective, was another pot of conversational gold, and the mood stayed identical across all three nights.

I took up a safe space in front of the sound desk, the sold out venue being packed tightly any further forwards, and the band duly arrived, surprising everyone, possibly half of the band themselves, by opening with "Cold War", a slower number from the first album, promoted up the running order as a "We're back in the USA 38 years later and look, the same shit's happening" type statement designed to span the gap in time. I felt a prod in the back and a shrill northern "What the bloody hell are they starting with this one for? No-one's bloody moving" in my ear as I grinned back and told her not to worry, I was sure it was designed as a mood-builder ready to explode into "Secret Noise". "Anyway," I reasoned, "how would I know, he's your husband, not mine!"

Branka tutted, barging her way towards the stage, presumably in order to adopt some form of conducting role, but before she could have got there, the band did indeed lead into their more traditional set opener, and collective heads from front to back of the hall hit the ceiling as one.

The excitement and crowd adoration went unabated through the night, with the set being altered from the now traditional UK staple to include more songs from the second album, and which were a joy to hear performed. All of the "New Clear Days" classics were of course still there, with the remainder of the set combining a rotation of the remaining tracks from that album and some new songs, different ones of each category appearing on each of the three nights.

The set closed in the usual style, and it would be safe to say that there wasn't a disappointed fan in the room, and there may not have been many dry eyes either. I had found it genuinely interesting the night before, gently people-watching the subtle but definite differences in how The Damned's American audience had behaved in comparison with their English counterparts. Watching this contrast play out in amplified form because this time it was The Vapors playing proved even more fascinating.

Despite her careful nurturing, coaxing, coaching and managing of Dave's pre-gig nervousness you can, as they say, take the girl out of Yorkshire, but you can't take the Yorkshire out of the girl. Branka thought they could do better, perhaps not quite having forgiven them all night for the perceived slow start.

"I'll give them a bollocking when I have to" she chirpily admits. "That first night in New York, I went straight to the dressing room afterwards and told them 'you were shit!'" Clearly surprising Michael with her over-exaggeration who looked at her quizzically, she continued "Well maybe not shit, but Dave spent half the evening with his eyes closed and his back to the audience, Dan thought he was bloody Dave Grohl, and none of you spoke to the bloody audience all night!" Brushing away protestations, and any hint of an excuse about jet lag, she finished making her point and instructed them to "Get up to the merch stand and meet some bloody fans!".

To return to a theme, was this the greatest gig the band had ever played? No. Was it nevertheless excellent and loved, as one, by the audience that night? Yes. That's more than good enough for me, but once again the sense of professionalism that drives the band when they perform was the most important thing in their minds, individual motives perhaps being slightly different, but the end desire being the same.

The band duly joined fans in the bar, and many a treasured item from long held home collections were brought out of bags for autographs, many photos were taken, and many shared drinks, conversations, and new associations spanning the Atlantic were made. In sharp contrast to the majority of UK gig venues, there was no rush to clear the crowd and send them home, and the party continued until well into the small hours of the morning.

Having to be back at the venue in late afternoon for the soundcheck on both of the subsequent days, and with most of the party flying back to the UK the day after the last show, sightseeing had to be managed according to personal requirement. Shaun, Jacqui, Tim, Mandy, the band and partners met a few of us back at Remedy Diner for the necessity of the all-American breakfast experience on the Saturday morning. Michael's eating exploits and prowess had by now become the stuff of band folklore, but the wide-eyed, childlike wonder on his face as everyone's piled high breakfast of choice arrived and he quizzed us all in turn "Wowwwww, what have you got there?" sticks firmly in the mind, as we all gleefully provided detailed descriptions of the constituent parts of treats such as crab cakes egg benedict served with chipotle hollandaise as they arrived one by one. It seemed very likely that he'd return the following morning and order the whole lot for himself.

Individual preferences for the day ahead, based on timescales and levels of alertness, were decided upon, and various groups formed to head off and tick off some of the obligatory, and some of the more off the beaten track, attractions that New York City has to offer. Having reasoned to myself that my restricted walking speed would hinder any of the others who had a faster paced requirement to cram in as much as they could during a single weekend, I had already decided to arm myself with a week-long subway pass and stay out a few days longer to do things at my pace. I love New York as much as any other city I have ever visited, so it seemed too good an opportunity to miss and to extend the trip rather than spend the most of it inside a music club. So I set off across Central Park, down 5th Avenue, past the Rockefeller Center and down to Times Square, stopping for occasional coffee and looking upwards, whilst the others headed off to The Empire State Building, The Statue of

Liberty, and a group headed over to the edge of the Hudson River, to walk The High Line, an atmospheric city-scaped path that runs on a raised and long dismantled goods railway. I'd like to have joined in with the latter, having loved the experience when I had previously visited the city, but my lack of mobility made it impractical. Although I probably covered the same distance that day, and every subsequent day, I genuinely enjoyed doing so with my enforced lack of haste contrasting perfectly with the never-ending rush of Manhattan whizzing by.

With the day used up, it was back to the hotel and then straight out, back to Benson's for pre-Vapors drinks part 2. We were greeted like old friends by the bar team, who knew already what we'd all want to drink, and settled down to discuss our days and look forward to gig number 2. We were joined by more US fans, and the atmosphere of expectation quickly built to at least the level it had reached the previous evening before we made our way around the corner.

There were again three bands on the bill that night, with the second act being Bobby Weiss's, also featuring his son Jack, a young Bobby with hair, lots of hair, and they struck a Ramones-like vibe that if it had needed to get the audience going would have done so, but by then the audience were pretty much going already, and stayed there all night.

Whether it was Branka's post-gig Friday bollocking, whether it was simply the band settling in and relaxing, or whether as is quite often the case, the second night was just better than the first as they got back into a rhythm after a gap between gigs, it was undoubtedly a classic. Most of the people who were at all three, band included, say that they felt that the third night was better still. From a musicianship point of view that may be true, but from my point of view the second night topped the lot. Although all three gigs were sold out, the venue seemed fullest on the Saturday night, and it was very much a Saturday night crowd. The whooping and the whistling and the dancing was unsurpassed and the atmosphere it created was simply magnificent. Dave had obviously also heeded Branka's advice when it came to a more relaxed crowd interaction, throwing in quips and anecdotes aplenty, and I felt the customary mid-gig Yorkshire poke in the back on one of her swans around the auditorium as she gesticulated towards Dave and noted "He thinks he's turned into chuffing Tommy Cooper!"

Another late-night party followed before an exhausted stagger back to the hotel.

More sightseeing ensued the following morning, and a now well-worn return to Benson's and into the venue, this time accompanied by an old college friend I hadn't seen since 1985, now based in New York and with whom I had been connected through a mutual Facebook friend. The gig did have a Sunday night feel to it, there is no doubt about that, but only in the sense that it was a bit more chilled, however it was certainly delivered with no less expertise. There was only one support band that night, The Split Squad again, and as a consequence the gig finished slightly earlier than on the previous two nights. There was no hanging around in the bar this time, however, as there was an after-show party booked at a location just around the corner, and any pretence of a Sunday night wind-down was blown away until the early hours of Monday morning. With the band finally able to relax, it turned into a jubilant celebration of a successful climax to all of the planning with bands, crew, management, families, fans and the heroes who had made the whole thing possible letting any hair they still possessed down in equal measures.

I've asked Evan how he felt the moment the band first came on stage on the first night, but he says "To be honest, at that point, I was so busy just running around, working so hard, making sure everyone had what they needed, setting things out in the dressing room that I don't remember the start of the show. I had family there, I just wasn't relaxed really. But that was OK. I'd seen them at the 229, I'd seen them at the soundcheck in the afternoon, the band were all relaxed and dressed down at that point and that was the moment when I thought 'don't blink, this is really happening, we made this happen.'" He qualifies this, detailing, justifiably that "Once they were playing though, I looked at the crowd, feeling so proud that they were all there enjoying it, jumping around, happy, drinking…that was exciting for me. That was the time I knew I'd achieved something important."

Both Evan and Bobby talk of "Full Circle" moments brought about by the return of The Vapors to the US, less in terms of the band's rebirth, but more personally related to linking those formative teenage memories fostered during their early, growing love of music and specifically this band to the glorious, nearly four decades on, affirmation of that link. For Bobby, he mentions a very specific point on the Sunday night when Jack and he were downstairs in the backstage room. "Steve and Dave got guitars out and were warming up with 'Somehow.' I didn't want to interfere, but I couldn't help myself. I started singing along. Just softly.

And I thought wow, with having Jack there as well, boy, what an outcome to all those years of wondering."

The wind-down came on the Monday, to an extent, with the majority of the UK contingent due to fly back that evening. Arrangements were made to meet in a classic Little Italy restaurant, now known as The Mulberry Street Bar, which is steeped in movie tradition having been used for filming in "Godfather III", "Night In the City" and "Donnie Brasco" amongst others, and was supposedly a favourite haunt of Frank Sinatra. Elaine and Jane had stumbled across the small restaurant earlier in the weekend, with its classic red and white checked tablecloths and a long, high-stooled bar running across the length of one side, and Jane suggested a last afternoon rendezvous there for anyone who fancied coming along, and I got there early to find Elaine, Jane, Matt and Sarah propping up the bar. Asked if we'd like a table, we declined saying that we weren't sure how many were coming along and would therefore wait awhile. We entertained ourselves, flicking through the wall-based CD jukebox which, to our delight, we discovered included not one, but two Vapors singles.

Gradually, various Vapors, various wives and partners, Tim, Mandy, Jim Fenton and his family, and indeed the full contingent of UK travelling fans, showed up in dribs and drabs. And once a few had arrived we decided to grab a table, which the restaurant quickly had to turn into several tables pushed together as more people arrived. By the time everyone had assembled, we had occupied every seat in the restaurant, apart from one small table where a couple of early diners sat and must have wondered if they'd walked into someone's private party. Matt timed his moment, being our nominated jester, and slotted a dollar into the jukebox, resulting in a high level "Turning Japanese" emerging from the sound of the speakers drowned out only by laughter and the groans of the band.

Alcohol was, of course, involved but so was classic New York Italian food served in the sort of quantity that ran the risk of satisfying even Michael's appetite, and it was a long, perfect afternoon that closed a long, perfect weekend. Steve remembers the afternoon with pride. "Yeah, that was something special, it felt like we had a real, y'know, crew out there with us, all weekend really but that afternoon sealed it and I thought 'all these people are here, thousands of miles from home, because of my band.' Awesome." He also laughs out loud when he recalls the piles of food arriving from the kitchen spread over all of our tables, "And I thought I'd use the opportunity to teach Michael about the concept of sharing. It was a non-starter really!"

Steve stayed in the bar with Rob, Rich and a couple of others right up until the time he had to get back to the hotel and leave for the airport, whilst a number of us, still trying stubbornly to minimise our alcohol intake, took one more stroll around the streets. Michael decided he needed to go back to the venue, as he wanted a photo of himself outside it to use when back on teaching duties in Brighton, and so we all headed back there for the required snaps to be attained. Having walked back to the scene of the weekend's triumph, Branka suggested the only realistic way possible of spending the last couple of hours and ushered us back around the corner into Benson's to be met with a mixture of mirth and disbelief.

"I thought we'd seen the last of you!" laughed the manageress. "So did I!" I replied. "But look, this time we've brought the band!" Dave, Michael and Dan were instantly given a heroes' welcome by the owner, seated at the bar and supplied with drinks on the house, and we truly did wind down before everyone else had to begin their homeward journeys. I retreated to the hotel, hitting the sack at about 8.00pm and waking up about fourteen hours later.

I spent another three days ticking off sites and curiosities, combining obvious activities like the boat trip around Manhattan and to The Statue Of Liberty with equally enjoyable but less obvious trips like wandering around grand, leafy suburbs of Brooklyn and up to the Brooklyn Bridge along the eastern side of the East River. I flew home exhausted, but incredibly fulfilled.

The challenge for the band, of course, was to follow that. That they managed to do so was quite some achievement. The previous year's Portmeirion show had been deliberately planned to be a little different, however heavy snow had fallen across most of Wales and the western half of England preventing some people getting there at all and making it very difficult for those that did make it. Despite that, it had been a great success, so a return was planned for 2018, a little earlier in the year this time. Unlike the previous year when I had been unable to attend due to illness anyway, this time I made it, courtesy of a lift with Owen and Jacquie after picking another of our number, Carol, up at Woking for an early start.

New York was indeed going to be a tough act to follow, but if you're going to do it, do it in style. Whereas pretty much every Vapors gig, ever, had been notable for the company, the music and quite often the atmosphere as well, sometimes, the physical characteristics of each venue's interior or location had played a major part. New York had taken that to another level for obvious reasons. So perhaps setting the next gig amongst the late autumnal colours of the Welsh mountains as they roll down to the sea, on the edge of a beautiful estuary, in a unique village setting, was a masterstroke.

The weekend was another success, with Owen, Jacquie and I staying in the "Castell Deudraeth" hotel built within an early Victorian mansion constructed in the style of a castle for added atmosphere. We met with the band for dinner in the hotel's restaurant shortly after we arrived and were retired to the on-site cottage they had hired as a group for drinks. Various relaxed tomfoolery followed, the highlight of which was watching Ed attempting to instigate an impromptu Punch and Judy show with Steve through the 70s-style serving hatch that linked the kitchen with the dining area of the house, something it was clearly designed for.

Another happy Vapors-related reunion bombshell was about to drop, however, as Sally sat down on the sofa next to me and fixed me firmly in the eye and said slowly and deliberately "So, Michael Philpott…"

"Blimey!" I replied sensing something portentous was about to happen "Only my mum calls me Michael."

"I bet you were known as Michael at school though," she continued mysteriously before continuing, "where did you grow up?"

I gave her a brief history of my story before she grinned widely. "Thought so, I've not met many Philpotts."

"It is him!" she yelled to Steve whilst I was still trying to make the connection before she turned back to me with a huge, half challenging, half amused smile. Sally, the Sally that had met Steve in the 90s when their paths had crossed working together at The Orange Club, was the same Sally that had taken that same early inspiration as I had from her class teacher, Mr Turner, at the age of 10. She was the same Sally with whom I'd passed through school and sixth form college, without ever really associating with her. To my embarrassment I didn't remember her at first, but as she began to recount her friendship groups and names were thrown around it began to fall into place. She had largely associated with a different crowd to mine, some of whom I remember, some of whom I vaguely recall, and some of whom I have no memory, but who I am quite sure would themselves be just as great company as Sally is if our paths ever crossed again.

We unpicked the tortuous routes that had led to us becoming modern day Vapors regulars, as I recounted to Sally's bemusement how I used to bunk off lessons to go and see the partner she would not meet until nearly twenty years later play bass guitar in his band. Sally explained how, like so many others, all she had known of The Vapors had been "Turning Japanese" until she met Steve in the 90s, her own musical tastes having been very different back then, but detailed the story of how they met at The Orange Club. Needless to say there were a few recounted memories and questions for each other during the rest of the weekend, as there have been ever since.

Most of the weekend was then spent wandering around the village, drinking coffee, eating lunch and enjoying another extended Vapors Family get-together, but the Sally bombshell had me shaking my head in amused disbelief for the remainder of the stay.

Oh yeah, and The Vapors played a gig on the Saturday night and it was great.

Three more gigs wound down the year, a brief South Coast spree that took in Margate on a Friday night and another almost hometown gig in Lewes on the Saturday night, for which Kev flew over and Pete travelled down. A number of us went back to Steve and Sally's for a very long session afterwards which Beccy and I ducked out of at 3.00 in the morning, but Kev and Pete saw through till daylight, Kev apparently then going back to his mum's on the Sunday morning and waking up at Monday lunchtime. Still got it.

Branka gave me a lift to that final show of the year, in Southampton, on that cold winter's Sunday evening, in theory another wind-down show but in practice another stormer, with the band on top form and Steve somehow shaking off his hangover to rock in style, a feat at which he is still apparently very competent.

Quantifying the best year of Vapors fanaticism from my point of view is difficult, if not impossible. The sheer joy of their discovery in 1979 and the association with every other aspect of my music world forty years ago? The repeated Marquee gigs and breakthrough into the popular eye in 1980? The tour, the familiarity and the exploits of 1981? Or maybe the sheer emotion of the reunion and the subsequent high profile shows in 2016 and the first half of 2017? Impossible to say, but the way 2018 was rounded off made it as good a candidate for that accolade as any.

Here Comes The Judge

In the first half of 2019, the band played an assorted mishmash of gigs across the UK at various festivals, and retro mod all-dayers, the only real highlight being a memorable support slot with Stiff Little Fingers and Eddie and the Hot Rods at one of London's stalwart and most iconic venues, The Forum in Kentish Town. With the untimely loss of the latter's Barrie Masters, literally at the time of writing, coming so soon after the loss of Pete Shelley, no further reminder should be necessary for those of us of a certain age and musical tendency to keep doing it, and to keep supporting these people that make it all so spectacularly wonderful.

In the spring, having secured the services of legendary producer Steve Levine, they headed to his studio in Liverpool to finally realise Dave's long-held dream, the recording of the third album. By this point the band had created and rehearsed over twenty new songs, and via a process that by all accounts combined a complex Eurovision style voting system with random smoke signals similar to those seen above the Vatican during the election of a new pope, producer and band whittled down the number to twelve for commitment to posterity. Ed and Dan shared guitar duties, with all writing being credited to the band in its entirety, all five members having created the sounds around Dave's lyrical observations – now less those of a concerned young man puzzling over women and the state of the world - more of a reflective, largely contented, life-experienced man puzzling over modern day issues, reflecting on a successful journey and continuing to worry about the state of the world.

During April, a post appeared on the Facebook page from a fan named Suzanne, recalling how she had travelled from her hometown of Cambridge in 1981 to Watford for her first Vapors gig. Reasoning that there was unlikely to be more than one such person who would fit this account, a final piece of the reformation jigsaw began to be placed for me. We met at the very busy "Mods Mayday" event at Islington Town Hall, where Owen and myself were doing a shift on the merch stall, and I overheard her mentioning to him that she had first seen the band in Watford on the "Mad March" tour. "Are you Suzanne?" I asked, which with hindsight would probably have taken her aback somewhat as she wouldn't have had the faintest idea who I was, but she confirmed that she was indeed one of the glove puppet quartet. We had more time to chat later in the summer at The Stone Valley festival, where she had travelled for the weekend, for which I will always be grateful as her camper van produced shelter from the early evening torrential downpour, and we reminisced all day about the end of The Vapors' career, other bands whose gigs we subsequently attended together, and of course the other girls. Suzanne had stayed friends with Streatham Sarah, who I learnt had tragically passed away when just thirty. I was of course upset to learn the reality, but I think subconsciously I was expecting it, there being simply no other rational explanation as to why she wouldn't have surfaced in The Vapors' world at some point after the reunion. We haven't, at this point at least, reconnected with Julie, but Suzanne and Melissa remain friends.

Elaine was able to square the circle of our seemingly certain acquaintance four decades ago when we chatted over the summer and she supplemented the visual records of her scrapbook with the production of her late 70s and early 80s diary. There, in black and white, was the evidence that we must have met. Not only did it contain names and addresses of all four glove puppet girls, Sarah's and Julie's details being so familiar to my eyes, but also an entry stating how in March 1981 "I got to The Venue in Victoria really early, where we met four girls called Sarah, Julie, Suzanne and Melissa and went into the soundcheck with them. We spent the whole evening with them and their friends." Kev, Colin and I, of course, were amongst that number, and Elaine's notes continue "Then we all went backstage to the dressing room to meet the band afterwards" which I remember clearly doing with the girls and a couple of others, which the documented evidence now clearly shows included Elaine. Final recognition was completed when Elaine's entry for that last Guildford Vapors gig, at The Royal, noted how she "Met the others outside the pub, wearing my famous red jeans", stirring my head into a hitherto long-dormant recollection of someone I vaguely remembered as "The girl with the red jeans" we'd met at the Victoria show.

In late July of this year the band headed off to the USA for the second time in a year, this time as part of a six week "Lost 80s Live" package tour that travelled countrywide and featured a number of disparate 80s acts playing nostalgia-fests in mid-sized halls and large outdoor arenas to audiences of a certain age. With neither Ed nor Dan available to tour, the band recruited the first American Vapor, Michael Giblin, a distinguished musician with a long CV and the driving force behind The Split Squad, to slot in effortlessly with lead guitar duties. Michael was therefore already well known to the band, fitted the bill perfectly, and is described by Steve as a "kindred spirit" which, knowing Steve, implies that the playing (non-musical) will have been at least as hard as the working throughout the whole road trip. Being a well-travelled musician, and American, Michael also assumed a large amount of the Tour Manager responsibilities in the US, being Shaun's man on the ground for the bulk of the tour and carrying out driving responsibilities when plane trips between shows weren't viable.

I decided a lot earlier in the year that making the trip to the US for this particular tour, with its huge distances, and in some cases long time lapses between shows, its short "highlights" set, and the general expense, made it an unrealistic proposition. I sat back and watched the lads post regular Facebook photos and stories, not just of the gigs and huge shows they were playing, but which also conveyed the sheer joy they were obviously experiencing on their cross-US road trip. I spoke with Branka a few weeks into the tour who confessed "I've cracked, I'm going to go to Vegas for the last show." As ever, being in absolutely no way a sucker to peer pressure, I responded with "Alright, I'll come with you", and we hatched plans to fly out for a long weekend, and at her instigation, to surprise Dave by not letting him know in advance that she was coming. Shaun helped with hotel and flight details, having already decided to fly out himself and also surprise the band for the last three shows, and we booked ourselves into the same hotel that the band would be using in Las Vegas, and on the same flight as them back to Heathrow the following day. Sally had made a similar decision, flying out to meet Steve in Los Angeles for the penultimate gig and travelling with the band to Vegas, and suddenly we had a three-day plot, which was implemented to perfection.

Vapors fan Jen Krost Adolph, a Florida resident as grand and brash as her name, whom we had all met last year in New York, made her own plans to cross the country with her sister Cindy and meet us there, and before we even left home we had a tourist itinerary that would keep us busy during the 36 hours between our arrival and that of the band in town.

A painless flight from Heathrow ensued, whilst Jen and her sister had a slightly more arduous experience travelling from Florida in the aftermath of Hurricane Dorian, with flight delays causing the missing of their connection, a subsequent rebooking and a generally stressful journey, but we all ended up at McCarran airport in Las Vegas at the same time, for which Branka and I were truly grateful as Jen had arranged to rent a car and was promptly able to drive us straight to our hotel.

A night of attempted jet-lag conquering bar crawling and burger consumption in Downtown Vegas followed, and the following morning featured a drive out to the desert courtesy of Jen and her rented car, which was a wonderful gesture and led to an incredible morning in the heat of the Valley Of Fire State Park. We spent three hours taking in a spectacular landscape that is just something that I would never have experienced without this impromptu weekend 10000-mile round trip and Jen's generosity.

The day wore on and Branka grew increasingly nervous about detection as Dave, sound checking in LA and clearly in range of a Wi-fi network called a couple of times on WhatsApp throwing Branka into a ball of confusion as we tried to reason what time it was back home, and therefore what Dave assumed she might be doing, and therefore what she should reply in her text that she should say she was up to. It was clearly too risky to answer the phone or indeed to call back, because the background noise was totally Vegas, and not at all curled up on the sofa Worthing, and it couldn't be masked. A text was therefore sent back apologising for missing the call, stating that an early night was being taken because she was going to get up on Saturday to drive to see her friend Barbie in Eastbourne, and wishing Dave good luck for that night's gig.

We spent an evening traversing The Strip in Vegas because, well you have to really. A lot is said and written about the place, and many readers will have roamed it themselves. All I'll say is wow. But never again.

The next morning came and the nerves were beginning to fray. In a partial recreation of my pre-Dublin gig nervousness I began to feel for Branka, still wondering if we might be discovered, but also slightly concerned about how Dave might actually react. We headed out for breakfast, settled down and ordered coffee when Branka's phone rang. "Fuck, fuck, fuck" she shouted, realising it was Dave and ignoring it. It rang again. And again. "Think Mike!" she begged, "What should I do?!" In the end, she answered her own question, texted Dave to apologise for not answering but explained that she was driving back from Barbie's in Eastbourne and that her battery was nearly dead, suggesting he rang her when he got to his hotel in Vegas. "OK will do, last night's gig was great" he replied, and we almost enjoyed our breakfast.

Having pulled on a Vapors T-shirt for the day, I was accosted as we left the diner, not for the last time that day, by a couple of American Vapors fans, of whom there seemed to be many roaming the immediate area, who discussed excitedly the songs they hoped that they would hear that night. They shared their first memories of the band, and listened in amazement as we told how we'd flown out from London just for the show, and so on, whilst Branka and I both implored each other mentally not to reveal identities, just in case they got straight onto Facebook and posted that they'd just met Dave Fenton's wife in Las Vegas. We were three hours away from the band's scheduled arrival, but as I began to feel like a very incompetent James Bond, we decided that safety would be the best option and Branka retreated to her hotel room whilst I hid in Starbucks.

The time approached and Shaun kept us posted as to their progress on the drive from LA, having now joined up with them himself. To our frustration, they stopped halfway, at Peggy Sue's Diner for a large breakfast which, with Michael Bowes in tow, would certainly not have been rushed, prolonging our agony. Finally, our convoluted system of lookouts, featuring Jen keeping an eye at the hotel's parking valet bay, relaying signals to Cindy and her husband who himself had flown in from Florida the previous night, who in turn sent semaphore to Branka and myself perched slightly uncomfortably on stools at fruit machines in the hotel's reception area, informed us of the party's arrival.

Shaun leapt ahead, scouting the area and noting Branka's location in the manner of a secret agent far more convincing than anything I'd been able to keep together earlier, before returning to the band making their slower entry with their luggage. Putting an arm round Dave and encouraging him to put his bag down, he escorted him around the corner where he couldn't miss the sudden and unexpected arrival of his wife. To everyone's relief and a great deal of applause it turned into a happy moment of surprised and elated reunion, and it had all been worth it.

We spent a relaxed afternoon in the bar before the band went off to prepare and I finally got some sleep after 60 hours of flying, nervousness, tourism, eye-boggling disbelief, excitement and time difference problems with virtually none, before wandering over to the show, already well underway, opposite the hotel in a large, open air arena that featured 16 bands that night as the end of tour finale.

The atmosphere was like none I'd ever experienced, certainly, and unsurprisingly very different to the sweaty confines of The Mercury Lounge a year previously, and closer to the feel of large outdoor shows in Hyde Park or elsewhere in the UK than anything else I'd ever been to, but very much in the middle of Las Vegas.

Knowing that I'd never seen The Vapors in surroundings remotely similar, and was unlikely to again, I elected to stand at the rear of the 8000 strong crowd and watch the short greatest hits set from an entirely different perspective, gazing in wonder at the tiny man in the stripy shirt and that bassist, and that drummer, 5000 miles from home, from hundreds of yards away, whilst trying to make out what I could of Mike Giblin's guitar playing, a new Vapors experience for me.

Watching Dave's face appear on giant video screens on either side of the stage was a truly weird moment.

A long night followed, taking in some of the other bands and socialising, and a painfully short night's sleep followed thanks to my staunchly defiant body clock.

The following day featured a mini-repeat of the New York weekend's Monday afternoon Italian restaurant experience in a craft beer brewery and bar around the corner, with band, UK tourists and Florida tourists alike, all having a couple of afternoon drinks and relaxing, for some of us after three days of enjoyment, and for some of us after six weeks of graft and exhaustion, but which clearly had also been exhilarating. I caught up with Mike Giblin, asking him how it had been to be a Vapor, and he replied simply "Y'know, before I left, my partner said to me 'Don't worry, you've only got to get one thing right for six weeks. No pressure, but don't fuck up that "da na na na na na na naaaa…" bit at the start of Turning Japanese.' I guess I didn't, so it's been a blast." It clearly had been.

Before we knew it, we were back to the airport and almost as painlessly back at Heathrow. As we sat in a cab on a damp, dreary drive back round the M25, Dave turned to Branka and unwittingly added the weekend's final surreal moment. "So how was Barbie in Eastbourne then?" he asked. As Branka laughed at him and chastised him good-naturedly for his stupidity I wondered briefly in my exhausted but contented state if actually his was the authentic reality, and whether the whole weekend had just been a dream.

******

At the time of writing, the new album is almost ready for release and will coincide with a long tour supporting Bruce Foxton's From The Jam, celebrating the 40th anniversary of the "Setting Sons" album, and its corresponding 1979 tour which started this whole thing off. There will be a third return to Portmeirion as part of the 40th anniversary celebrations, this time a full weekend Vapors convention, with fans committed to attending from all over the world, and more shows supporting From The Jam after Christmas and into the spring. Plans for any further activity have yet to be made, and who knows what may happen, but there's certainly plenty of clamour on both sides of the Atlantic for more.

I'm particularly interested in how Dan sees his musical future, assuming that he'll be playing for considerably longer than the others. Other than the prospect of forming some bizarre punk version of "S Club Juniors" with other Vapors' offspring (not an altogether outlandish idea) he states with the common sense learned from goodness knows where that "I'd like to get all my qualifications in order first, have something I can always fall back on, and then have a real crack at the music." Given that he has another three years of study before he completes his PhD it would seem that the public may have to wait a while yet, but he is on the verge of putting another band together in Cardiff to keep him occupied in idle moments and keep the fingers in shape. What's happened already isn't lost on him. "New York was so surreal. 'Sold Out' is just something they put on the poster but walking from the back of that packed room to the stage with my wireless gear on ready to pick up the guitar and play, with all those people cheering and whistling and pointing at me, that was just gobsmacking. I really had no words. I knew what 'Sold Out' meant then. I don't think I'll ever experience anything like that" he says, echoing what a lot of us in our 50s and 60s may (and indeed did) say, but sounding almost sad coming from someone only in their mid-twenties. "Yeah but I always strive for more, for better", he continues with a comfortable but not arrogant confidence.

I'm still a music fan. That part of me has ebbed and flowed for the whole of my life and was certainly on the rise again in the years leading up to the rebirth of the band. But the opportunity to once again follow The Vapors to venues up and down the country (and beyond), and the social circle and excitement it has spawned, has recreated perfectly a contented, comfortable middle-aged version of the teenage fanaticism that the same band first engendered within me back in 1980.

Unlike many similar gig goers, I'm not a big collector. For sure, I have a collection of records, but I'm definitely not a record collector. I don't keep ticket stubs or maintain Excel spreadsheets detailing gig attendance. Merchandising T-shirts, when occasionally acquired, are worn till old and tatty and then discarded (most often only when there are too many to fit into the drawer and my wife's patience has snapped with their continued, scruffy presence). I have an original pair of 1980 red, white and blue Jam shoes in the attic, and possibly a shoe box full of button badges from that era, but that is all.

But I collect special memories in my head, and music helps me replay them. Long may that faculty remain. There's a place in my mind where I occasionally wash up, a brief, off the scale emotional sense of euphoria, triggered when a feeling echoes timelessly down the ages through my senses, sparked by something that I am listening to. Apart from the aural stimulation, what hits like lightning is a long bygone, but somehow briefly touchable, glorious sense of a still mentally reachable time and place (Marquee club, Brighton Alhambra, front of a crowded Jam gig). Very few bands' music takes me there, and even when it does, it's a very rare feeling. But The Vapors' back catalogue has always on occasion managed to, and now, 38 years after the release of their last recorded material, new music from the same band is, it seems, going to be capable of doing the same.

What happens next is anyone's guess. If it all ends tomorrow, it will do so with an unequivocal, unanimous ringing endorsement from fans everywhere for resurrecting, in such a memorable way, a band that meant so much to us all so long ago. Above and beyond that, some critical acclaim for what promises to be a hugely accomplished new album based upon the evidence offered by the new songs that have already been performed, that will certainly be unmistakably The Vapors but unmistakably contemporary, would be welcomed by band and fans alike, as undoubtedly would be some commercial success. And if the band carry on for years to come with the same ability, drive, camaraderie and surrounded by such a wonderful community, then even better.

Proper 21st century contact has been established via Facebook, Twitter and Instagram, as well as the Vapors fans' Facebook group that has become such a central point of reference for us all. Thevapors.co.uk website has recently gone live, with Owen's expertise based on his years of experience running The Stranglers' equivalent being put to good use and giving him the opportunity to lovingly maintain more lists of stuff, an invaluable gig history amongst them.

Evan, Bobby and others have all described those "Full Circle" moments in relation to specific personal episodes related to this group, the former also voicing his opinion that the upcoming "From The Jam" tour may represent something similar for the band. Somewhere during the past three years, or maybe spanned across all of them, is my own personal equivalent. Or maybe, it came just recently, directly as a result of, but not immediately involving, the association with The Vapors that I treasure so deeply. After the band had played the Vegas set, I engaged in a short moment of tomfoolery dancing around my walking stick and pirouetting around Dave as we "Wang Chunged" to another of the bands on the 80s line-up from much later in the decade (who turned out, surprisingly to my punk purist mind, to be excellent). We then retreated to the backstage area where many of the night's line-up were milling around, socialising and comparing notes after six weeks of bonding and touring together, but tellingly climbing the stairs to support each other from behind the stage as the remaining bands played their sets.

My mind wandered back to 1977, and the tiny transistor radio stuffed down the side of my bed drifting in and out of tune with Radio Luxembourg as it brought me strange, new sounds from around the world. An early memory from that time was of punk/glam/rock band The Tubes, just starting out on their career and sounding mystical and wondrous to me as they were introduced as coming from the West Coast of the USA, a country whose geography back then I had such little knowledge of that such a location could have been anywhere in the world, or beyond for that matter. As the same band climbed to the stage to perform in Las Vegas, Steve grabbed me round the shoulder and said "Come on Mike, we should go and watch these, they've been great on this tour", and we clambered up the same stairs behind them. I watched in awe and wonder with Steve from the back of the stage as that band, one of the earliest memories of my musical awakening that I retain, played, 42 years later, to 8000 people stretched out in front of us in the Nevada night.

Deep breath.

It's been an absolute joy to have been immersed in The Vapors and their music during a critical part of my teenage development, to have had their sound and the memories wrapped around me ever since, to have had the pleasure to be so involved with the reboot and the upgrade since 2016, and above all to be able to so proudly call the band, their families and so many fans, old and new, my friends.

We all have our ups and downs of course, but in my middle-aged comfort, as I reflect on a life pretty well negotiated thus far, and as I look forward to growing as old and disgracefully as my wife will tolerate and my doctors will allow, it's great to have you all around.

Thanks lads.

48633729R00152

Printed in Poland
by Amazon Fulfillment
Poland Sp. z o.o., Wrocław